TERRELL ON THE LAW OF PATENTS

TERRELL ON THE LAW OF PATENTS

FIRST SUPPLEMENT TO THE EIGHTEENTH EDITION

SWEET & MAXWELL  THOMSON REUTERS

Eighteenth Edition (2016) by Sir Colin Birss, Douglas Campbell QC, Tom Mitcheson QC, Tom Hinchliffe QC, Justin Turner QC and Andrew Waugh QC

Published in 2017 by Thomson Reuters (Professional) UK Limited, trading as Sweet & Maxwell.

Registered in England & Wales. Company number 1679046. Registered office 5 Canada Square, Canary Wharf, London E14 5AQ.

For further information on our products and services, visit
www.sweetandmaxwell.co.uk

Printed and bound in Great Britain by CPI Group (UK) Ltd, Croydon, CR0 4YY

No natural forests were destroyed to make this product; only farmed timber was used and re-planted.

A CIP catalogue record of this book is available from the British Library.

ISBN: 9780414062320

PREVIOUS EDITIONS

First Edition (1884) by Thomas Terrell

Second Edition (1889) by Thomas Terrell

Third Edition (1895) by W.P. Rylands

Fourth Edition (1906) by Courtney Terrell

Fifth Edition (1909) by Courtney Terrell

Sixth Edition (1921) by Courtney Terrell and A.D. Jaffe

Seventh Edition (1927) by Courtney Terrell and D.H. Corsellis

Eighth Edition (1934) by J.R. Jones

Ninth Edition (1951) by K.E. Shelley KC

Tenth Edition (1961) by K.E. Shelley QC

Eleventh Edition (1965) by Guy Aldous QC, Douglas Falconer and William Aldous

Twelfth Edition (1971) by Douglas Falconer QC William Aldous and David Young

Thirteenth Edition (1982) by William Aldous QC, David Young QC, A. Watson and S. Thorley

Fourteenth Edition (1994) by David Young QC, Antony Watson QC, Simon Thorley QC and Richard Miller

Fifteenth Edition (2000) by Simon Thorley QC, Richard Miller QC, Guy Burkill and Colin Birss

Sixteenth Edition (2006) by Simon Thorley QC, Richard Miller QC, Guy Burkill QC, Colin Birss and Douglas Campbell

Seventeenth Edition (2011) by Richard Miller QC, Guy Burkill QC, Colin Birss QC and Douglas Campbell

PREFACE

This work marks another major change for *Terrell*, the first ever supplement. It is hard to believe how much has happened since the main work was published. With the Court of Appeal deciding *Warner-Lambert v Actavis*; the law relating to second medical use claims and plausibility continues to develop. The EPO has clarified the law on partial and poisonous priority in G1/15. In terms of practice and procedure, in *Positec v Husqvarna* and *Illumina v Premaitha*, the High Court has addressed disclosure in patent cases, while the pilot Shorter Trial Scheme has started and has been used in the Patents Court.

The main work included a chapter on the UPC on the apparently uncontroversial basis that the court was likely to start during the currency of the edition. Since the referendum result in June 2016 the likelihood of the UPC coming into existence has varied somewhat, so we will make no predictions. The UPC chapter is in the main work, so we have tried to keep it up to date.

The whole editorial board have contributed to the supplement and again Georgina Messenger deserves our thanks for marshalling the materials. Douglas Campbell QC deserves a special mention for his dedication to getting this supplement done on time and as accurately as we can manage.

We have tried to state the law as of 1 January 2017.

C.B.
Middle Temple
1 March 2017

HOW TO USE THIS SUPPLEMENT

This is the First Supplement to the Eighteenth Edition of *Terrell Law of Patents* and has been compiled according to the structure of the main volume.

At the beginning of each chapter of this Supplement, a mini table of contents of the sections in the main volume has been included. Where a heading in this table of contents has been marked by the symbol ■ there is relevant information in this Supplement to which you should refer.

Within each chapter, updating information is referenced to the relevant paragraph in the main volume.

TABLE OF CONTENTS

TABLE OF CASES

TABLE OF EPO DECISIONS

(References are to paragraph numbers)

DECISIONS OF THE ENLARGED BOARD OF APPEAL (G NOS)

TABLE OF STATUTES

(References are to paragraph numbers)

TABLE OF STATUTORY INSTRUMENTS

(References are to paragraph numbers)

TABLE OF CIVIL PROCEDURE RULES

(References are to paragraph numbers)

TABLE OF CIVIL PROCEDURE RULES - PRACTICE DIRECTIONS

(References are to paragraph numbers)

TABLE OF EUROPEAN AND INTERNATIONAL TREATIES AND CONVENTIONS

(References are to paragraph numbers)

TABLE OF EU LEGISLATION

(References are to paragraph numbers)

PATENTS

CONTENTS

4. INTERNATIONAL CONVENTIONS

The TRIPS Agreement

Replace paragraph with:

The TRIPS Agreement was signed by the UK and by the Council of the EU on **1-73** which all Member States of the EU are represented. It has also been ratified by the Council of the EU (see Council Decision 94/800/EEC) and, under UK national law, it is to be regarded as a Community Treaty as defined in s.1(2) of the European Communities Act 1972. [145] However, it is clear that the TRIPS Agreement is not directly applicable in Member States of the EU. [146] Nevertheless the ECJ has held that, in a field to which TRIPS applies and in respect of which the Community has already legislated, the judicial authorities of the Member States are required by virtue of Community law, when called upon to apply national rules falling within that field, to do so as far as possible in the light of the wording and purpose of TRIPS. [147] Note that the CJEU has also held that the EU has exclusive competence in the interpretation of the TRIPS Agreement—see *Daiichi Sankyo* and *Sanofi-Aventis Deutschland* (C-414/11).

[145] The European Communities (Definition of Treaties) (The Agreement Establishing the World Trade Organisation) Order 1995 (SI 1995/265).

[146] *Parfums Christian Dior SA v Tuk Consultancy BV* (C-300-/98 and C-392/98) [2000] E.C.R. I-11307; [2001] E.T.M.R. 26, [44]; *Monsanto Technology LLC v Cefetra BV* (C-428/08) (Grand Chamber, 6 July 2010), [71]. See also *Azrak-Hamway International Inc's Licence of Right (Design Right and Copyright) Application* [1997] R.P.C. 134; *C-G Lenzing A.G.'s European Patent* [1997] R.P.C. 245.

[147] *Hermès International v FHT Marketing Choice BV* (C-53/96) [1998] E.C.R. I-3603, [1998] E.T.M.R. 425; *Parfums Christian Dior SA v Tuk Consultancy BV* (C-300-/98 and C-392/98) [2000] E.C.R. I-11307, [2001] E.T.M.R. 26; *Schieving-Nijstad VOF v Groeneveld* (C-89/99) [2001] E.C.R. I-5851, [2002] F.S.R. 22; *Merck Genéricos—Produtos Farmacêuticos* (C-431/05) [2007] E.C.R. I-7001, [35]; *Monsanto Technology LLC v Cefetra BV* (C-428/08) (Grand Chamber, 6 July 2010), [77]. And see also *Nova Productions Ltd v Mazooma Games Ltd* [2007] E.M.L.R. 14, [37]; *Experience Hendrix LLC v Purple Haze Records Ltd* [2008] E.M.L.R. 10, [27]–[28]; *Supreme Petfoods v Henry Bell & Co* [2015] E.T.M.R. 20, [48]–[49]. See also para.1-77, et seq.

Agreement on a Unified Patent Court

After "19 February 2013.", add:

1-89   On 28 November 2016 the UK indicated that it would ratify the Agreement irrespective of the referendum result on 23 June 2016.

CHAPTER 2

THE NATURE OF PATENTABLE INVENTIONS

CONTENTS

3. INDUSTRIAL APPLICABILITY

Add new paragraph:

In *Epshtein v Comptroller-General of Patents Designs and Trade Marks* [24a] Roger **2-22a**
Wyand QC (sitting as a Deputy High Court Judge) allowed an appeal against a
Hearing Officer's rejection of 11 patent applications on the ground that they lacked
industrial applicability. The claims related to the treatment of various conditions using dosage forms prepared from solutions of ultra-low dilutions of antibodies (i.e.
diluted to such a degree that, statistically speaking, the solutions did not contain a
single molecule of the original antibody). The Hearing Officer had held that data
resulting from double-blind placebo-controlled studies which had been appropriately performed established that a therapeutic effect was plausible but that
without any explanation of the mechanism behind the therapeutic effect the data
should be rejected on the basis of placebo effect and experimental anomalies.
However, the Deputy Judge held that if the plausibility of the therapeutic effect is
established by data then, even if the reason for it cannot be explained, the claim is
plausible (see [55]). He also held that this was so even though the claimed effects
were difficult to believe (see [58]).

[24a] [2016] EWHC 1511 (Ch).

[3]

ENTITLEMENT

CONTENTS

4. ENTITLEMENT PROCEEDINGS

Entitlement jurisdiction

Comptroller declining to deal with a case

Add new paragraph: **4-56a**

The appeal from the Comptroller in *NGPOD Global Ltd v Aspirate N Go Ltd* [144a] was concerned with a decision refusing to decline to deal with a case under s.37(8). The appeal was allowed because the entitlement dispute raised significant non-patent law issues which were significantly beyond the likely experience of a hearing officer, including estoppel, employment law, contract law, company law and insolvency law. The court also rejected a submission that s.37(8) allowed for a two-stage consideration of the matter whereby a hearing officer could determine that a dispute should properly be heard in the High Court as a first stage but, because of the word "may", could still sensibly not decline to deal with it. Mann J held (at [14]):

> "For my part I find it hard to imagine how a hearing officer could decide that a case is more properly tried in the High Court but still refuse to decline to deal with it. Such a refusal would seem to me to be perverse. The overriding objective will have been taken into account at the first stage of the reasoning. In line with other courts in other cases, I suppose I should never say never, but it does strike me that the "may" encompasses a purely theoretical discretion. In any event, as I have observed, nothing in this appeal seems to turn on it."

[144a] [2016] EWHC 3124 (Pat).

THE GRANTED PATENT

CONTENTS

6.   PATENT OFFICE OPINIONS

Comptroller's power to revoke

Add to end of paragraph:

This discretion was exercised for the first time in February 2016 in relation to   **5-99**
where all the claims in a patent were found to lack novelty or inventive step. [237a]

[237a] Opinion no. 04/15 dated 4 June 2015; Fujifilm Corporation's European patent.

CHAPTER 6

SUPPLEMENTARY PROTECTION CERTIFICATES

CONTENTS

2. THE APPLICATION FOR A CERTIFICATE

Date by which an application must be made—art.7

Replace paragraph with:

Thus the time for a UK applicant which runs under art.7(1) does not start even **6-38** if that applicant has obtained a marketing authorisation elsewhere in the Community. The time under art.7(1) only starts to run once a authorisation applicable to the UK has been granted. This was part of the problem confronted by the applicant in the *Yamanouchi* case.[78] In that case, on the date of its application on 15 January 1993 the applicant had obtained a marketing authorisation in France but its application in the UK had been delayed. It was not ultimately granted until 1995. However, the patent expired on 17 January 1993. Thus if the applicant had waited until 1995 to make the application under art.7(1) within six months of the date of the UK application, then the patent would have expired two years beforehand and art.3(a) would not have been satisfied. The applicant therefore tried to bring its application under the then transitional provisions (art.19) but that attempt failed as well on the basis that the court held that there had to be a local authorisation in place. This issue was revisited in *Merck Sharp & Dohme Corporation v The Comptroller-General of Patents, Designs and Trade Marks*.[78a] In that case the patent was due to expire before the relevant marketing authorisation had been granted through the decentralised procedure. Instead the applicant applied for a certificate based on the notice of grant (end of procedure notice). Both the UKIPO and the judge thought that this meant that art.7 had not been complied with and could not be rectified under art.10(3) of the Medicinal Products Regulation. Arnold J has nevertheless referred questions to the CJEU (Case C-567/16) to clarify whether the end of procedure notice was to be treated as equivalent to a granted marketing authorisation, and if not, whether the absence of a granted marketing authorisation at the date of the application was an irregularity that could be cured under art.10(3) once the marketing authorisation had been granted.

[78] *Yamanouchi Pharmaceuticals Co Ltd v C-G* (C-110/95) [1997] R.P.C. 844.

[78a] [2016] EWHC 1896 (Pat).

Add new paragraph:

6-39a   The consequences for certificates granted prior to the decision in *Seattle Genetics* remains unclear. In *Incyte Corporation & Szellemi Tulajdon Nemzeti Hivatala (National Intellectual Property Office)* the Hungarian Court has asked the CJEU to clarify whether, (a) if the "date of the first authorisation to place the product on the market in the Community" is incorrect, where that date was determined without taking account of the judgment in Seattle Genetics, and (b) it is appropriate to rectify the date of expiry of the supplementary protection certificate even if the decision to grant that certificate was made prior to that judgment and the time limit for appealing against that decision has already expired? It also asked whether the industrial property authorities of Member States were required to rectify, of their own motion, the date of expiry of certificates in order to ensure that that they comply with *Seattle Genetics*.

3.   SUBSTANTIVE CONDITIONS FOR THE GRANT OF A CERTIFICATE

"Product"

Excipients

6-71a   *Add new paragraph:*
    See also *Abraxis Bioscience LLC v The Comptroller General of Patents*[139a] where Arnold J dismissed an appeal from the UKIPO under art.1(b). The certificate sought was for "paclitaxel formulated as albumin bound nanoparticles"—referred to as "nab paclitaxel". Paclitaxel was a well-known anti-cancer drug and had previously received marketing authorisations in the EU. The applicant submitted that its formulation of nab-paclitaxel represented a new single active ingredient and the evidence showed that nab-paclitaxel was more effective and safer than paclitaxel. Following a comprehensive review of the CJEU cases on excipients, Arnold J concluded that it was clear that nab-paclitaxel was not the active ingredient within the meaning of art.1(b): paclitaxel was the active ingredient and albumin was merely a carrier. He refused a reference under art.1(b) because he considered that the law was clear—art.1(b) should be interpreted narrowly and an active ingredient is a substance which produces a pharmacological, immunological or metabolic effect on its own.

[139a] [2017] EWHC 14 (Pat).

An appropriate and valid authorisation to place the product on the market has been granted

(art.3(b) Medicinal Products Regulation/art.3(1)(b) Plant Protection Regulation)

Replace paragraph with:

6-102   The appropriate authorisation under art.3(b) is a local one, i.e. an authorisation in the UK. That can be seen by reading art.3(b) with the preamble in art.3 overall which states "in the Member State in which the application is submitted". An authorisation elsewhere in the Community, although potentially relevant for determining the overall period of validity of any certificate under art.13, is not relevant under art.3(b) and there must be a valid authorisation in the UK at the date of the application.[198] The authorisation referred to in art.3(b) must be of the appropriate kind, i.e. one granted in accordance with Directive 65/65 (now Directive 2001/83/EC) since art.3(b) says as much in express terms. But see the reference made in *Merck Sharp & Dohme Corporation v The Comptroller-General of Patents, Designs and Trade Marks* [198a] which asks whether the end of procedure notice in the decentralised procedure was to be treated as equivalent to a granted marketing authorisation.

[198] *Yamanouchi Pharmaceuticals Co Ltd v C-G* (C-110/95) [1997] R.P.C. 844.

[198a] [2016] EWHC 1896 (Pat).

The relevant authorisation is the first authorisation to place the product on the market as a medicinal/plant protection product

(art.3(d) Medicinal Products Regulation/art.3(1)(d) Plant Protection Regulation)

Add new paragraph:

The decision in *Neurim* was revisited in *Abraxis Bioscience LLC v The Comptroller General of Patents.* [217a] The certificate sought was for "paclitaxel formulated as albumin bound nanoparticles"—referred to as "nab paclitaxel". The applicant contended that nab-paclitaxel was a new formulation of paclitaxel. In the light of *Neurim* it submitted that art.3(d) was to be interpreted as meaning that the authorisation referred to in art.3(b) was the first relevant authorisation, i.e. the first authorisation within the scope of the basic patent, to place the product on the market as a medicinal product. Further, it suggested that although *Neurim* was a case about a new therapeutic use of an old active ingredient, the same policy considerations should apply to a new formulation of an old active ingredient. Arnold J. did not agree and considered that it would be inconsistent with a strict interpretation of art.1(b) to interpret art.3(d) as permitting certificates to be granted for new formulations of old active ingredients. However, he did not consider the matter to be acte clair, and accordingly has referred the issue to the CJEU. **6-114a**

[217a] [2017] EWHC 14 (Pat).

Cases which concern combinations of active ingredients

Add new paragraph:

The Gilead case revisited

The *Gilead* case referred to at paras 6-125 and 6-126 returned to the High Court in 2016 when a number of generic companies challenged its validity in the light of the ensuing CJEU case-law referred to above. The challenge was based on the second of the two points previously determined by Kitchin J. It was said that art.3(a) of the Medicinal Products Regulation was not satisfied for a combination product of tenofovir and emtricitabine when the relevant claim of the basic patent (claim 27) referred only to "tenofovir and optionally other therapeutic ingredients". In his judgment in *Teva UK Ltd v Gilead Sciences Inc* Arnold J carried out a comprehensive review of all the art.3(a) case law, and held that whilst it was clear that what he termed the Infringing Act Rules were not sufficient to satisfy art.3(a), it was not clear whether what he termed the Extent of Protection Rules were sufficient. He therefore felt it necessary to refer once more to the CJEU the question "What are the criteria for deciding whether 'the product is protected by a basic patent in force' **6-150a** in art.3(a) of the SPC Regulation?" The judge's own view was that satisfying the Extent of Protection Rules was not sufficient for art.3(a) and that the product must go further and contain an active ingredient, or a combination of active ingredients, which embodied the inventive advance (or technical contribution) of the basic patent. Where the product was a combination of active ingredients, the combination, as distinct from one of them, must itself embody the inventive advance of the basic patent.

4. EFFECTS OF A CERTIFICATE

Duration of the certificate

Replace paragraph with:

6-172   The first Community authorisation for the purposes of calculating the duration under art.13 only has to authorise marketing somewhere within the Community (or EEA), it need not permit free circulation of the product throughout the Community. This issue was decided in *Novartis*. [305] Here the applicant applied for a certificate in the UK. The UKIPO contended that an authorisation granted by Switzerland but effective in Lichtenstein as a result of Lichtenstein law was the relevant first authorisation for the purposes of calculating the duration of the certificate under art.13. Although Switzerland was not part of the EEA, Lichtenstein was. The issue was referred to the Court of Justice and was heard with a similar case referred from the courts in Luxembourg. The Court of Justice decided that the Swiss authorisation which was effective to authorise marketing in Lichtenstein was the relevant first authorisation in one of the states of the EEA within the meaning of art.13. The deciding factor was that this must be correct because otherwise there would be a risk that the period of 15 years of exclusivity would be exceeded in the EEA. [306] The fact that the authorisation effective in part of the EEA (Lichtenstein) did not permit the product to be freely distributed on the market of the other Member States was not relevant since even authorisations granted in one state under the relevant European law (Directive 65/65, etc.) do not permit the product to be freely distributed. [307] The CJEU affirmed its decision in *Novartis* in its reasoned order in *Astrazeneca*. [308] See also *F. Hoffmann-La Roche AG v Accord Healthcare OU* (C-572/15) where the CJEU confirmed that where the certificate had been issued in a state prior to its accession to the EU (in that case, Croatia), the first marketing authorisation for the purposes of art.13 was still the first authorisation in the EEA.

[305] *Novartis AG, University College London and Institute of Microbiology and Epidemiology v Comptroller* (C-207/03) conjoined with *Ministre de l'économie v Millenium Pharmaceuticals Inc* (C-252/03).

[306] *Novartis AG, University College London and Institute of Microbiology and Epidemiology v Comptroller* (C-207/03) conjoined with *Ministre de l'économie v Millenium Pharmaceuticals Inc* (C-252/03), [31].

[307] *Novartis AG, University College London and Institute of Microbiology and Epidemiology v Comptroller* (C-207/03) conjoined with *Ministre de l'économie v Millenium Pharmaceuticals Inc* (C-252/03), [32].

[308] *Astrazeneca AB v Comptroller General of Patents, Designs and Trade Marks* (617/12).

5.   THE PAEDIATRIC EXTENSION OF THE DURATION OF A CERTIFICATE

Application for a paediatric extension

Curing irregularity in the application

Replace paragraph with:

Article 10(3) of the Medicinal Products Regulation gives the Comptroller the   **6-182**
power to ask the applicant to rectify irregularities in an application within a stated
time. In *E I Du Pont Nemours & Co v UKIPO*[321] the problem facing the applicant
was that by the end of the period within which an application could be made, the
formal conditions required to grant the extension were not satisfied but they were
clearly going to be satisfied soon, albeit probably after the last date on which an application could be made, but nevertheless before the end of the extension (if
granted). Therefore, asking for an extension was well worthwhile. The applicant
made an application for an extension within the time set by art.7(5) and then sought
a period within which to rectify the "irregularity" in its application. The "irregularity" in the application was that neither of the two documents required were or could
be provided at the date of the application. The application did not have a copy of
the statement required by art.8(1)(d)(i) nor proof that the product was authorised
in all Member States as required by art.8(1)(d)(ii); the reason why not being the
same in both cases namely that as at the date of application there was no such statement nor was the product authorised across all Member States as required. The
UKIPO purported to set a date for the irregularities to be cured but also stated that
the defects were incurable. The Court of Appeal ruled that the defects were irregularities within art.10(3), they could be cured and the right thing to do was to
set a date by which the documents had to be provided. By the time the case had
reached the Court of Appeal the defects had been cured and the Court's decision
was that the UKIPO could extend the supplementary protection certificate. This is
to be contrasted with the decision of Arnold J in *Merck Sharp & Dohme Corporation v The Comptroller-General of Patents, Designs and Trade Marks* where he
determined that a deficiency under art.7(1) to grant a supplementary protection
certificate could not be rectified under art.10(3). However, he held that the answer
he had given was not acte clair and has referred the issue to the CJEU.

[321]   [2009] EWCA Civ 966; [2010] R.P.C. 6.

Date for assessing criteria for grant

Replace paragraph with:

The *E I Du Pont Nemours & Co* decision is significant since its effect is that the   **6-183**
date on which the criteria for grant of an extension have to be satisfied is not the
date of the application for the extension and is not limited by requirements in art.7
for the date by which an application must be made. While this is undoubtedly a
pragmatic decision in the circumstances it remains to be seen whether the same approach might be extended to applications for basic supplementary protection
certificates themselves. The problem in the *Yamanouchi* case[322] was similar to that
faced by *E I Du Pont Nemours* —at the last date on which the rules provided that
Yamanouchi could apply for a supplementary protection certificate they did not and
could not satisfy the criteria for grant of a certificate because they had no UK
marketing authorisation. They had applied for one and would get it in future before
the end of the period which the certificate would have covered if granted. However,

Yamanouchi did not obtain a certificate. Similarly the Comptroller's Hearing Officer refused a certificate in *Merck Sharp & Dohme Corporation's Application*[323] where an "End of Procedure Communication of Approval" had been received from the Reference Member State at the date of application but not formal approval for marketing authorisation. This decision was upheld on appeal (*Merck Sharp & Dohme Corporation v The Comptroller-General of Patents, Designs and Trade Marks*[323a]), but Arnold J considered that the issues arising were not acte clair and has referred them to the CJEU.

[322] *Yamanouchi Pharmaceuticals Co Ltd v C-G* (C-110/95) [1997] R.P.C. 844.

[323] BL O/117/16.

[323a] [2016] EWHC 1896 (Pat).

PRIORITY DATE

CONTENTS

2.   THE BASIC RULE AND THE RIGHT OF PRIORITY

Successor in title

Replace paragraph with:

    In *Idenix Pharmaceuticals v Gilead Sciences*,[26] the Court of Appeal confirmed   **7-14**
that where the priority of the cited prior art is challenged, by way of defence to a
validity attack, the usual principles as to entitlement to priority apply. In *Idenix*, this
included US law evidence as to the validity of assignment of the invention, and the
Court held that the approach of Arnold J that equitable title was sufficient (see also
KCI Licensing v Smith & Nephew[26a]) was the correct approach under English law.

[26] [2016] EWCA Civ 1089.

[26a] [2010] FSR 31.

Add new paragraph:

    The question of which party bears the burden of proving entitlement to priority   **7-14a**
of an item of prior art which did not derive from either party arose in *Actavis Group
v ICOS Corporation & Eli Lilly*.[26b] Although the legal burden of proof will lie on
the party relying on the citation, in most cases there will be an evidential burden
on the patentee to rebut the inference which can be drawn from the claim to priority on the face of the document. The patentee should make clear well before trial
whether it is going to take the point.

[26b] [2016] EWHC 1955 (Pat).

3.   PRIORITY—THE TEST

Priority in English law

Add to end of paragraph: **7-28**

    In the same manner, the requirement of plausibility will apply to questions of
priority as well as sufficiency—*Hospira UK Limited v Cubist Pharmaceuticals
LLC*.[49a]

[49a] [2016] EWHC 1285 (Pat), [114]–[123].

Priority document must disclose the claimed invention

Replace paragraph with:

7-29   Assessment of entitlement to priority must therefore be made not only with the disclosure of the priority document but also with the scope of the invention of the claims in mind. In *Hospira UK Limited v Cubist Pharmaceuticals LLC*,[49b] Carr J rejected the patentee's submission that this meant that only the "key concept" of the invention need be disclosed. The correct approach, following G2/98, was to take a narrow and strict interpretation of the "same invention". Simply because the patent contains additional information not present in the priority document does not mean that the claims are not entitled to priority. Further, it is frequently the case that a priority document will be filed without claims and in such a specification the various features found in the claim of the granted patent are unlikely to be written out together in a neat paragraph.[50]

[49b] [2016] EWHC 1285 (Pat).

[50] As was the case in *Hospira UK Limited v Genentech Inc* [2014] EWHC 1094 (Pat).

Selection of sub-class

Add new fn.63a after "However, the fact that it is a narrower range does not mean that there is support for that range.":

7-33   [63a] See *Hospira UK Limited v Cubist Pharmaceuticals LLC* [2016] EWHC 1285 (Pat), [120]–[123].

4.   MULTIPLE AND PARTIAL PRIORITIES

Partial priority and poisonous priorities

Add new paragraph:

7-50   The Enlarged Board of Appeal issued a ruling[82] in reference G1/15 which indicates that an approach to partial priority will be taken which would put an end to poisonous priorities. The reasons for the ruling have not yet been published. The ruling states:

> "Under the EPC, entitlement to partial priority may not be refused for a claim encompassing alternative subject-matter by virtue of one or more generic expressions or otherwise (generic 'OR'-claim) provided that said alternative subject-matter has been disclosed for the first time, directly, or at least implicitly, unambiguously and in an enabling manner in the priority document. No other substantive conditions or limitations apply in this respect."

[82] Dated 29 November 2016.

Add new paragraph:

7-51   The reasoning of G1/15 is set out in section 6 of the decision and, in particular, at [6.4]–[6.7]:

> "6.4 In assessing whether a subject-matter within a generic 'OR' claim may enjoy partial priority, the first step is to determine the subject-matter disclosed in the priority document that is relevant, i.e. relevant in respect of prior art disclosed in the priority interval. This is to be done in accordance with the disclosure test laid down in the conclusion of G 2/98 and on the basis of explanations put forward by the applicant or patent proprietor to support his claim to priority, in order to show what the skilled person would have been able to derive from the priority document. The next step is to examine whether this subject-matter is encom-

passed by the claim of the application or patent claiming said priority. If the answer is yes, the claim is de facto conceptually divided into two parts, the first corresponding to the invention disclosed directly and unambiguously in the priority document, the second being the remaining part of the subsequent generic 'OR'-claim not enjoying this priority but itself giving rise to a right to priority, as laid down in Article 88(3) EPC.

6.5 This also corresponds, logically and exactly, to the scheme described in the Memorandum (see point 5.2 above): 'If a first priority document discloses a feature A, and a second priority document discloses a feature B for use as an alternative to feature A, then a claim of the application directed to A or B will in fact consist of two distinct parts A and B respectively, each complete in itself ...', and further: '... it would be appropriate to claim a partial priority in situations corresponding to the "OR"-situation under "Multiple Priorities", the European patent application itself taking the place of the second priority document'.

6.6 The task of determining what is the relevant disclosure of the priority document taken as a whole, and whether that subject-matter is encompassed by the claim in the subsequent application, is common practice in the "EPO" and among practitioners of the European patent system and as such should not pose any additional difficulty. Nor does it create uncertainty for third parties, as argued by the respondent and in some amicus curiae briefs. Although it can be a demanding intellectual exercise, the decisions reached in cases T 665/00, T 135/01, T 571/10 and T1222/11 all show that it can be carried out without any need for additional tests or steps.

6.7 From this analysis it follows that the assessment of entitlement to partial priority right does not show that any additional requirements are needed."

CHAPTER 8

THE "PERSON SKILLED IN THE ART" AND COMMON GENERAL KNOWLEDGE

CONTENTS

1. THE "PERSON SKILLED IN THE ART"

Is the "person skilled in the art" the same for all such purposes?

Replace fn.11 with:

[11] See, e.g. *JALON/Luminescent Security Fibres* (T422/93). See also the judge's summary of the arguments in *Accord Healthcare Ltd v Medac Gesellschaft Für Klinische Spezialpraparate Mbh* [2016] EWHC 24 (Pat), [14]–[15].

8-19

Replace quotation with:

"I think the flaw in that is to assume that 'the art' is necessarily the same both before and after the invention is made. The assumption may be correct in most cases, but some inventions are themselves art changing. If a patentee says 'marry the skills of two different arts to solve a problem,' marrying may be obvious or it may not. If it is not, and doing so results in a real technical advance then the patentee deserves and ought to have, a patent. His vision is out of the ordinary.

8-20

This is not because a different construction is being given to the phrase 'person skilled in the art' in the different Articles. It is because the phrase is being applied to different situations. Where the issue is claim construction or sufficiency one is considering a post-patent situation where the person skilled in the art has the patent in hand to tell him how to perform the invention and what the monopoly claimed is. But ex-hypothesi the person skilled in the art does not have the patent when considering obviousness and 'the art' may be different if the invention of the patent itself is art changing.

In the case of obviousness in view of the state of the art, a key question is generally 'what problem was the patentee trying to solve?' That leads one in turn to consider the art in which the problem in fact lay. It is the notional team in that art which is the relevant team making up the person skilled in the art. If it would be obvious to that team to bring in different expertise, then the invention will nonetheless be obvious. Likewise if the possessor of the "extra expertise" would himself know of the other team's problem. But if it would not be obvious to either of the notional persons or teams alone and not obvious to either sort of team to bring in the other, then the invention cannot fairly be said to be obvious. As it was put in argument before us the possessors of the different skills need to be in the same room and the team with the problem must have some reason for telling the team who could solve it what the problem is."

Delete para.8-21.

Delete para.8-22.

"Person skilled in the art" may be a team

Replace fn.33 with:

8-35   [33] [2010] EWCA Civ 819, [41]. See also *Accord Healthcare Ltd v Medac Gesellschaft Fur Klinische Spezialpraparate Mbh* [2016] EWHC 24 (Pat), [16]–[18].

Replace fn.39 with:

8-37   [39] [2015] EWHC 2548 (Pat), [118]. See also *Actavis v Icos Corp* [2016] EWHC 1955 (Pat), [72]–[73].

Attributes of the person skilled in the art

Level of skill

Replace paragraph with:

8-44   The level of skill and training assumed of such a person may differ widely depending on the subject matter. There are technologies where no great knowledge is to be attributed to the skilled person and others (such as genetic engineering) where to attribute an unrealistically low level of attainment to the skilled person would prejudice industrial development.[46] In *Regeneron v Kymab*[46a] where the "skilled person" comprised a team including an immunologist with an interest in the production of therapeutic antibodies and a genetic engineer with an interest in the creation and development of transgenic animals, a submission that such persons could follow a protocol and exercise ordinary skill in making it work, but could not develop a new protocol, which would require creative problem-solving and inventiveness, was rejected. The skilled team would use common general knowledge and routine trial and error in an attempt to adapt an experimental protocol if it did not work. Nevertheless, the skilled team did not have the imagination or creative ability to solve problems that cannot be tackled by routine, iterative trial and error.

[46] *Glaxo Group's Patent* [2004] R.P.C. 43, [24].

[46a] [2016] EWHC 87 (Pat), [55]–[59].

CONSTRUCTION OF THE SPECIFICATION AND CLAIMS

4.   PURPOSIVE CONSTRUCTION IN PRACTICE

Replace heading with: **9-68**

Virgin v Premium: A practical working guide

Replace paragraph with:
The distilled principles adopted in *Virgin v Premium Aircraft*[68] are set out below: **9-70**

"Principles of claim construction

5.   One might have thought there was nothing more to say on this topic after *Kirin-Amgen v Hoechst Marion Roussel* [2005] RPC 9. The judge accurately set out the position, save that he used the old language of Art 69 EPC rather than that of the EPC 2000, a Convention now in force. The new language omits the terms of from Art. 69. No one suggested the amendment changes the meaning. We set out what the judge said, but using the language of the EPC 2000:

[182]The task for the court is to determine what the person skilled in the art would have understood the patentee to have been using the language of the claim to mean. The principles were summarised by Jacob LJ in *Mayne Pharma v Pharmacia Italia* [2005] EWCA Civ 137 and refined by Pumfrey J in *Halliburton v Smith International* [2005] EWHC 1623 (Pat) following their general approval by the House of Lords in *Kirin-Amgen v Hoechst Marion Roussel* [2005] RPC 9. An abbreviated version of them is as follows:

    (i)   The first overarching principle is that contained in Article 69 of the European Patent Convention;

    (ii)   Article 69 says that the extent of protection is determined by the claims. It goes on to say that the description and drawings shall be used to interpret the claims. In short the claims are to be construed in context

    (iii) It follows that the claims are to be construed purposively—the inventor's purpose being ascertained from the description and drawings.

(iv)   It further follows that the claims must not be construed as if they stood alone—the drawings and description only being used to resolve any ambiguity. Purpose is vital to the construction of claims.

(v)   When ascertaining the inventor's purpose, it must be remembered that he may have several purposes depending on the level of generality of his invention. Typically, for instance, an inventor may have one, generally more than one, specific embodiment as well as a generalised concept. But there is no presumption that the patentee necessarily intended the widest possible meaning consistent with his purpose be given to the words that he used: purpose and meaning are different.

(vi)   Thus purpose is not the be-all and end-all. One is still at the end of the day concerned with the meaning of the language used. Hence the other extreme of the Protocol—a mere guideline—is also ruled out by Article 69 itself. It is the terms of the claims which delineate the patentee's territory.

(vii)   It follows that if the patentee has included what is obviously a deliberate limitation in his claims, it must have a meaning. One cannot disregard obviously intentional elements.

(vii)   It also follows that where a patentee has used a word or phrase which, acontextually, might have a particular meaning (narrow or wide) it does not necessarily have that meaning in context.

(vii)   It further follows that there is no general 'doctrine of equivalents.'

(viii)   On the other hand purposive construction can lead to the conclusion that a technically trivial or minor difference between an element of a claim and the corresponding element of the alleged infringement nonetheless falls within the meaning of the element when read purposively. This is not because there is a doctrine of equivalents: it is because that is the fair way to read the claim in context.

(ix)   Finally purposive construction leads one to eschew the kind of meticulous verbal analysis which lawyers are too often tempted by their training to indulge."

[68] [2010] EWCA Civ 1062, [5].

Delete para.9-71.

Add new paragraph:

9-72a   In *Regeneron Pharmaceuticals Inc. v Kyman Ltd and Novo Nordisk A/S* [70a] Henry Carr J had to consider the meaning of the term "an in situ replacement" in the context of a claim for the genetic modification of mice. He adopted the approach he described at [149], et seq:

"149. In considering this issue, I shall apply the principles of construction as set out in *Virgin Atlantic Airways Ltd v Premium Aircraft Interiors UK Ltd* [2010] RPC 8 at [5]. The task for the Court is to determine what the person skilled in the art would have understood the patentee to have been using the language of the claim to mean. Furthermore, the claim must be construed without knowledge of the alleged infringement, as it does not change its meaning depending on the acts of the defendant. However, it is necessary to have in mind the issue(s) on infringement in order to focus on the points that are material. In *Technip France SA's Patent* [2004] RPC 46 Jacob LJ said: 'Although it has often been said that the question of construction does not depend on the alleged infringement ("as if we had to construe it before the defendant was born"...) questions of construction seldom arise in the abstract. That is why most sensible discussion of the meaning of language runs on the general lines "does it mean this, or that, or the other?" rather than the open-ended "what does it mean?'"

150. I shall also bear in mind the observations of Floyd LJ in *Adaptive Spectrum v British Telecommunications* [2014] EWCA Civ 1462: 'It must be remembered, however, that the specification and claims of the patent serve different purposes. The specification describes and illustrates the invention, the claims set out the limits of the monopoly which the patentee claims. As with the interpretation of any document, it is conceivable that a certain, limited, meaning may be implicit in the language of a claim, if that is the meaning that it would convey to a skilled person, even if that meaning is not spelled out expressly in the language. However it is not appropriate to read limitations into the claim solely on the ground that examples in the body of the specification have this or that feature. The reason is that the patentee may have deliberately chosen to claim more broadly than the specific examples, as he is fully entitled to do.'

151. The parties agree that the phrase 'in situ replacement' is not a term of art. Therefore, it is for the court to determine its meaning, but it needs to be educated in order to do so. In *Ultraframe UK Limited v Eurocell Building Plastics Ltd* [2005] RPC 36 at [5]–[7] Jacob LJ considered the principles of claim construction and in particular, what a person skilled in the art would have understood the patentee to have used the language of the claim to mean. At [7] he said: 'Before the court gets to the examination room it has to do some swotting: to get into its mind the relevant knowledge of the skilled man. For how a document will be understood depends on the reader.'"

[70a] [2016] EWHC 87 (Pat)..

Add new paragraph:

The principles of claims construction as set out in *Kirin-Amgen Inc v Hoescht*   **9-72b**
Marion Roussel Ltd,[70b] and in *Virgin Atlantic Airways Ltd v Premium Aircraft Interiors UK Ltd*[70c] were also applied in *GlaxoSmithKline UK Ltd v Wyeth Holdings LLC*.[70d]

"69. The essential question for the Court is to determine what the person skilled in the art would have understood the patentee to have been using the language of the claim to mean."

[70b] [2005] R.P.C. 9.

[70c] [2010] R.P.C. 8, [5].

[70d] [2016] EWHC 1045, [69], et seq.

8.   PARTICULAR FORMS OF CLAIM

"Swiss-style" or "use" claims

Add new paragraph:

The decision of Arnold J in *Warner-Lambert Co LLC v Generics UK Ltd*[314a] came   **9-283a**
before the Court of Appeal (Floyd, Kitchin and Patten LLJ).[314b] Because the Court of Appeal upheld the judgment of Arnold J on the issue of the invalidity of the patent in suit, it was not necessary for the Court of Appeal to revisit the issue of infringement. Nevertheless, as Floyd LJ held, (at [186]) in view of the judge's "obviously profound reservations" about the law, it would not have been right to leave the case without considering the principal arguments, even though they were no longer necessary for the Court of Appeal's decision. Floyd LJ observed at [187].

"187.The issue which this aspect of the case raises is, and remains, one of great difficulty. The law is struggling on the one hand to give the patentee a proper reward for his contribution to the art by elucidating the new use for the drug, whilst at the same time not excluding the competing manufacturer from making and marketing the drug for its known purpose. The issue is complicated by the interaction with the law relating to, and the practices of the market in, prescription medicines. The solution adopted by this court in *Warner-Lambert* CoA was an attempt to strike the right balance by not placing insuperable obstacles in the path of the patentee, whilst at the same time recognising in very clear terms that the remedies available for infringement will have to be moulded so as to achieve fair and proportionate relief tailored to the very special circumstances of this type of case."

[314a] [2015] EWHC 2548 (Pat).

[314b] See [2016] EWCA Civ 1006.

Add new paragraph:

9-283b   With that introduction, Floyd LJ turned to the substantive issue of Swiss-form claims at [189], et seq. Floyd LJ re-considered the cases he had previously considered and, in particular, the decision of the *Landgericht Hamburg in Warner-Lambert Company LLC v Aliud Pharma GmbH*. Having done so, he found at [191] that:

"The 'only packaging will do' approach has obvious advantages of practicality, but I remain very clearly of the view that it does not provide adequate protection for the patentee. I did not understand Mr Speck, who argued this part of the case for Actavis, to contend that we should rigidly follow the approach of the German courts. These matters arise as a matter of interpretation of the word 'for'. The parties are agreed that the word imports a mental element. Packaging may be a means of demonstrating the necessary mental element, whatever that is, but it cannot possibly be the only means of doing so."

Add new paragraph:

9-283c   Floyd LJ went on to consider (at [192]) a "somewhat wider approach" in Spain, where what is looked for is an express authorisation for the new indication or some other act of encouragement of the use for that indication (citing *Wyeth v Arafarma and Qualtec* (539/07), the Madrid Court of Appeal). Floyd LJ also considered the more recent French decision of the Tribunal de Grande Instance dated 26 October 2015 in *Warner-Lambert v Sandoz* (15/58725) (Judge Marie-Christine Courboulay) where the court, in summary proceedings, held that Warner-Lambert's claim for infringement was not sufficiently established. Floyd LJ also considered judgments in Denmark, Spain, France [314c] and the EPO and observed that:

"These cases continue to show a spectrum of different approaches. Some countries have gone for the "only packaging will do" approach. Some countries look more generally for some element of encouragement of the use of the drug for the new use by the manufacturer before being prepared to find infringement. Others look to see what steps have been put in place in the marketplace to prevent use for the prohibited indication. I do not think a universal principle has yet emerged."

[314c] As a post-script he also considered further judgments from France, Sweden and Spain; at [228]–[231].

Add new paragraph:

9-283d   After summarising the parties' submissions at [202]–[205] Floyd LJ concluded by saying that:

"206.I think the debate in this case has been distorted by reference to notions of subjective intention. I have no doubt that an objective approach is necessary. From an objective standpoint one would normally regard a person to intend what he knows or can reasonably foresee as the consequences of his actions. That is the test which I formulated in *Warner-Lambert* CoA."

207. If that is the basic test to be adopted, what is sufficient to negative the existence of intention? In my judgment the absence of the patented indication from the label cannot conceivably be sufficient to negative the intention. Mr Speck recognised that there could be objective factual circumstances where the absence of a label identifying the patented indication did not negative intention, for example a manufacturer who proposes to sell far more of the drug than the market for the non-patented indication could bear.

208. Viewed in this way I think the answer becomes clear. The intention will be negatived where the manufacturer has taken all reasonable steps within his power to prevent the consequences occurring. In such circumstances his true objective is a lawful one, and one would be entitled to say that the foreseen consequences were not intended, but were an unintended incident of his otherwise lawful activity. I think this approach is in line with that adopted in the decision of the Tribunal de Grande Instance, in that it recognises an obligation on the manufacturer to take steps if he is to enter the market where he stands to benefit from the patentee's contribution to the art."

Add new paragraph:

As considered in the section under infringement at para.14-24a, Floyd LJ **9-283e** considered that the judge fell into error in seeking to dissect the requirement for intentional treatment of pain in the way he did (i.e. as between the doctor on the one hand and the pharmacist on the other). Floyd LJ held (at [216]) that because Swiss-form claims rely for their novelty on the purpose of the use of the drug,

"...it is only essential that the manufacturer is able to foresee that there will be intentional use for the new medical indication. Intentional use is to be distinguished from use where the drug is prescribed for a different indication and, without it in any sense being the intention of the treatment, a pain condition is in fact treated."

[25]

CHAPTER 10

INVALIDITY AND THE GROUNDS OF REVOCATION

3. COMBINING THE INDIVIDUAL GROUNDS OF REVOCATION

Replace fn.34 with:

[34] See para.10-64 as regards "plausibility".

10-47

Validity and "squeeze" arguments

Add new heading and paragraph:

Costs implications of squeeze arguments

After a trial the court is frequently invited to discount the winning party's allow-
able costs on the grounds that some of its arguments failed. Where the losing arguments nevertheless formed part of a successful squeeze, such costs may still be
allowed: see *Hospira UK v Cubist Pharmaceuticals.*[47]

10-63

[47] [2016] 5 Costs LR 1011.

Add new heading and paragraph:

10-64

Plausibility

The question of whether a patent or priority document makes something
"plausible" has recently come up in the context of industrial application, sufficiency, priority, obviousness, and novelty (in particular, enablement). The term is
not to be found in the legislation and first came to prominence in the context of
industrial applicability and sufficiency in *Eli Lilly v Human Genome Sciences.*[48]
Since then it has been considered in the context of insufficiency by the Court of Appeal in *Regeneron Pharmaceuticals v Bayer Pharma,*[49] again in *Generics (UK) t/a
Mylan v Warner-Lambert Company LLC;*[50] and by the Court of Appeal in relation
to inventive step in *Generics (UK) Ltd v Yeda Research & Development Co*[51] and
again in *Idenix v Gilead.*[52] This growing body of case law has established that the
requirement of plausibility is a low, threshold test designed to prohibit speculative
claiming; and that the sense conveyed by the word is that there is some real reason
for supposing that the statement is true. It has also been held at first instance that
there is no distinct requirement for plausibility in the law of novelty, over and above
disclosure and enablement, but in a proper case plausibility is an aspect of
enablement. Specifically, in order to amount to an enabling disclosure of a medi-

[27]

cal use claim and thereby deprive the claim of novelty, the prior art has to make the therapeutic effect plausible.

[48] [2011] UKSC 51.

[49] [2013] R.P.C. 28, [95]–[103].

[50] [2016] EWCA Civ 1006, [46]–[47].

[51] [2014] R.P.C. 4, [36]–[49].

[52] [2016] EWCA Civ 1089, [104]–[114].

CHAPTER 11

INVALIDITY DUE TO LACK OF NOVELTY (ANTICIPATION)

CONTENTS

2.   SECTION 2(2): THE STATE OF THE ART

Add new paragraph:

A dispute as to whether a document formed part of the state of the art at all arose **11-13a**
in *Unwired Planet v Hauwei.*[3a] The question was whether a document uploaded
onto an internet server in Europe at 08.36 (which corresponded to 07.36 GMT) on
8 January 2008 constituted prior art with respect to a priority document filed at the
USPTO at 16.59 (which corresponded to 21.59 GMT) on 8 January 2008. It was
held that the relevant priority date was the one at the patent office where the priority document was filed; that a disclosure made on the same day as that priority date,
albeit earlier in time, was not prior art; and that time zones in different places around
the world were irrelevant.

[3a] [2015] EWHC 3366 (Pat).

(2)   To whom must the matter be made available?

Whether a disclosure is in fact confidential

Replace paragraph:

Examples

The above principles relating to implied obligations of confidentiality have been **11-36**
consistently applied in the English authorities addressing the question of "made
available to the public", where the question arises whether the recipient was "free
in law and equity" to make use of information disclosed to him. Some examples
are as follows:

(a)   In *Catnic v Evans*[27] (a case involving a patent granted under the 1949
      Act), an architect had shown a model lintel to several parties whom he
      hoped to interest in making it commercially, in the expectation (to their
      knowledge) of some reward if they did so. While he had not expressly
      bound them in confidence, it was held that they were under implied
      obligations of confidence. As a result, the lintel did not become "known"
      as a result of those disclosures.

(b)   In *Pall v Commercial Hydraulics*,[28] a case involving a patent under the
      1977 Act, Falconer J had to consider two alleged prior uses: (i) a supply

to a potential customer of experimental samples for a comparison test, and (ii) a supply to five other companies of samples for purposes of testing. In relation to use (i), he held that the samples were experimental and secret and that no details of their construction could have been determined; in the circumstances he held that there was not an "enabling disclosure" and thus no anticipation. As for (ii), he held that as the primary purpose for sending the experimental samples was to obtain testing feedback for further development into a commercial product, they were sent under conditions of confidence.

(c) In *Strix v Otter*,[29] the defendants relied on prior disclosures between Strix and Philips. Ferris J held that those parties had been acting pursuant to a joint venture in which there was a mutual obligation of confidence within the tests set out in *Coco v Clark*, which he expressly applied. Thus neither party was free to disseminate information provided to it by the other, and so there was no invalidating prior disclosure.

(d) In *Kavanagh Balloons v Cameron Balloons*,[30] HHJ Fysh similarly applied *Coco* and *Strix*.

(e) By contrast, in *BAYER/Plasterboard*[31] the patentee had before the priority date of its patent carried out experimentation at the premises of its customer. There was no formal development agreement and no formal *secrecy* agreement. An argument that secrecy should be assumed as the parties had a common interest in maintaining it was rejected; the Board of Appeal rejected this, holding that there was no common interest and thus no obligation of secrecy so that the patent was invalid.

(f) In *Aga Medical Corporation v Occultech (UK)*[32] Roth J held that no obligations of confidence applied to medical devices used in clinical trials conducted in Bratislava. This was despite the fact that the Opposition Division of the EPO had held that the same disclosure was confidential.[33]

(g) In *Eugen Seitz v KHS Corpoplast*[34] Roth J held that a fax sent by one defendant to the other nine years prior to the patent was written and intended to be viewed in the context of a joint project which neither defendant was free to disclose to third parties: hence it was confidential. In the same case an issue arose as to whether the supply of a particular machine from one to company (Soplar) to an independent company (Alpla) was done under conditions of confidence. The evidence showed that at the relevant time all of Soplar's machines were built for Alpla and that the companies' relationship was unusually close. Roth J nevertheless held that Alpla was under no obligation of confidence as regards the Soplar machines.

(h) In *Thoratec Europe Limited v AIS GmbH Aachen Innovative Solutions*[34a] it was held that the supply of a prior art catheter pump to a researcher in order to study its effect in animals was not confidential, and neither was the arrangement of the magnetic coupling used therein, hence such prior use deprived the patent of novelty.

Burden of proof for establishing "free in law and equity"

Replace fn.36 with:

³⁶ See especially *Dunlop* at 542/20–543/2. See also *Qualcomm v Nokia* [2008] EWHC 329 (Pat), at **11-39**
[113]. In *Thoratec Europe Limited v AIS GmbH Aachen Innovative Solutions* [2016] EWHC 2637 (Pat)
it was explained that whilst the legal burden lies on the party relying on a prior use of a product to
establish that the prior use made the construction of the product in question (so far as relevant) available to the public, the evidential burden of establishing confidentiality may shift to the other party.

Disclosure

Add new paragraph:

By contrast, in *Glaxosmithkline UK v Wyeth Holdings*[84a] the information **11-79a**
disclosed to the skilled addressee by the relevant prior art ("the Cuban vaccine")
did not anticipate since, inter alia, it was not shown that the ordinary skilled person
could identify the presence of the relevant protein ("fHbp") in the Cuban vaccine.

^{84a} [2016] EWHC 1045 (Ch).

"Inevitable results" must be strictly proved

Replace paragraph with:

Thus in *Inhale v Quadrant*[92] Laddie J held that even though it was "overwhelm- **11-85**
ingly likely" that the prior art had formed a composition within the claims of the
patent in suit, this was not enough for the purposes of anticipation: see below. In
BASF v SKB[93] Pumfrey J noted at [44] that the same test was also applied in the
EPO, the examination guidelines stating that the inevitable result objection should
only be raised where there "can be no reasonable doubt as to the practical effect of
the prior teaching".[94] In *Swarovski-Optik v Leica Camera*[95] the prior art device was
adjustable. In normal operation it did not anticipate the claim but it would do so if
adjusted to suit a set of unusual conditions. The argument was whether the possibility that it might be so adjusted was enough to establish anticipation. The Court of
Appeal doubted the legitimacy of this approach but did not find it necessary to
decide the issue. In *Thoratec Europe Limited v AIS GmbH Aachen Innovative Solutions*[95a] the court held that one item of prior art did not clearly and unmistakeably
disclose the magnetic clutch required by the claim: it was merely more likely than
the alternative friction coupling. The court also dismissed an "ingenious" argument that if such prior art was ambiguous then it disclosed both possibilities.

⁹² [2002] R.P.C. 21, [103]–[104].

⁹³ [2002] EWHC 1373, [44].

⁹⁴ See Part G, Chapter VI, at para.6 (November 2015 edn).

⁹⁵ [2014] EWCA Civ 637. See [103], [105] and [106].

^{95a} [2016] EWHC 2637 (Pat).

Add new paragraph:

However, as was pointed out in *Actavis v Teva (Tadalafil)*,[95b] one has to **11-85a**
distinguish between two different kinds of likelihood. In *Inhale v Quadrant*, Laddie J was not talking about the standard of proof in civil cases and nor were the
Houses of Lords in *General Tire* and *Synthon*. *Inhale* was a case in which the target
was not precisely defined in the prior art and it was not inevitable that a skilled
person would arrive at the target in the claim: in particular, it was overwhelmingly
likely that they would produce something with a Tg of at least 20°C but it was not
inevitable because a Tg of 19.5°C would have been sufficient for purposes of the

prior art. By contrast the Court in Tadalafil cited and applied Floyd J in *Actavis v Janssen*[95c] as follows:

> "406. The point on standard of proof came up in the Nebivolol case *Actavis v Janssen* [2008] FSR 35 . Here Floyd J had to decide if a product would have the relevant property. He held that it was overwhelmingly likely that it would and then said the following:
>
> > '85. Is that finding good enough for an inevitable result? The legal requirement is that this feature of the claim be the inevitable result of carrying out the prior teaching. Does that mean that if there is some other possibility, even a fairly remote one, that some other result would follow, I should conclude the result is not inevitable? Or am I concerned to establish what, on the balance of probabilities would in fact occur? In my judgment, it is the latter approach which is correct. The inevitable result test does not require proof of individual facts to a quasi-criminal standard. It may be impossible to establish the relevant technical facts to that standard. It is another matter if the evidence establishes that sometimes one result will follow and sometimes another, depending on what conditions are used. But there is nothing of that kind suggested here. It is simply a question of what occurs in fact.'
>
> 407. I respectfully agree. This is not in conflict with Inhale, it is concerned with a different question."

[95b] [2016] EWHC 1955 (Pat).

[95c] [2008] F.S.R. 35.

Add new paragraph:

11-85b   Hence although the evidence before the court in Tadalafil only went so far as an opinion that it was "highly likely" that the product would have the claimed property, the court found that that the product which would inevitably be produced would, as a matter of fact decided on the balance of probabilities, be within the relevant claims such that they lacked novelty.

Nature of experiments necessary to prove "inevitable results"

Add new footnote to end of sentence:

11-87   [97a] However, the discussion of *Inhale* and *Synthon* in this paragraph and the next should be read in the light of the discussion at para.11-85a.

5.   PARTICULAR FORMS OF CLAIM

Selection patents

Replace paragraph with:

11-134   Jacob LJ there noted that what an "individualised description" amounted to might involve questions of degree. (Contrast, e.g. *Ranbaxy v Warner-Lambert*[158] where the claim was held anticipated because alighting on the claimed compound was merely picking one of the class of compounds disclosed in the prior art, so that "if the claim were valid it would cover one of the alternatives explicitly taught by the citation".) For an illustration of one such matter of degree, see *Glaxosmithkline UK v Wyeth Holdings*[158a] at [157]–[169].

[158] [2007] R.P.C. 4, [40].

[158a] [2016] EWHC 1045 (Ch).

CHAPTER 12

INVALIDITY DUE TO OBVIOUSNESS (LACK OF INVENTIVE STEP)

CONTENTS

2.   OBVIOUSNESS—GENERAL PRINCIPLES

Obvious with respect to what?—The relevant "matter"

Mosaicing: combining cited art with other material

Replace fn.41 with:

[41]   [2010] EWHC 1487 (Pat), at [112] approved on appeal in [2010] EWCA Civ 1260.   **12-33**

Add new paragraph:

In *Richter Gedeon v Generics (UK) Ltd*[41a] the Court of Appeal reaffirmed its ap-   **12-33a**
proval of the passage from *KCI Licensing v Smith & Nephew* cited above. Jacob
LJ explained (at [23]) that he could not see any logical distinction between a case
where it is obvious to look something up and one where it is obvious to ask, and it
was obvious that the answer would be given and would be clear. The notional asking is exactly equivalent to the notional looking up. In both cases the prior art spurs
the action of finding out in a non-inventive way.

[41a]   [2016] EWCA Civ 410.

Obviousness over common general knowledge alone

Replace paragraph with:

In *Ratiopharm v Napp*[45] Floyd J noted that it was not the general practice to plead   **12-37**
the relevant common general knowledge relied upon in support of such a case but
considered that some formal exposition in advance of expert reports would be
appropriate. He then made a number of observations regarding the approach to be
taken to an allegation of obviousness over common general knowledge alone. The
first was self-evident: it is that it is essential that the starting point for the plea is
indeed established to be common general knowledge. Secondly, it is important to
be precise about what it is that is asserted to be common general knowledge; for
example it may be important to distinguish between knowledge of the existence of
a product and knowledge of particular applications. Thirdly, it is vital to have in
mind the requirements for matter to be part of the common general knowledge: see
in particular the passage in *Beloit v Valmet*,[46] discussed at para.8-66 of this work.

Fourthly, allegations of obviousness in the light of common general knowledge alone need to be treated with a certain amount of care. They can be favoured by parties attacking the patent because the starting point is not obviously encumbered with inconvenient details of the kind found in documentary disclosures, such as misleading directions or distracting context. It is vitally important to make sure that the whole picture presented by the common general knowledge is considered, and not a partial one.[47] Finally, the common general knowledge does not include knowledge which does not inform the skilled person's approach from the outset. The judge explained the final point thus:

"Whether knowledge is common and general depends on the considerations explained by Aldous LJ in *Beloit*. If information does not satisfy that criterion, it does not become common general knowledge by postulating a set of steps that the skilled team might take to find it if they had already embarked on an attempt to solve a particular problem. That is not to say that it is illegitimate, in assessing an obviousness attack, to take account of material which would inevitably be found and treated as reliable in consequence of a step or steps which it is obvious to take. If the material so found is such as would be accepted, then it may assist in showing obviousness of a further step. But what it cannot be used for is in support of an argument that the series of steps being undertaken were obvious from the start."

Further examples of cases where obviousness over common general knowledge alone was argued are *Unwired Planet v Huawei*[47a] in which the argument failed and *Sony Communications International AB v SSH Communications Security Corp*[47b] in which it succeeded.

[45] [2009] R.P.C. 11, [154]–[159]. See also *Nokia v Ipcom* [2009] EWHC 3482 (Pat), [109].

[46] [1997] R.P.C. 489, 494–5.

[47] These difficulties are well illustrated in *Accord Healthcare v Medac* [2016] EWHC 24 (Pat), see [119]–[124].

[47a] [2016] EWHC 576 (Pat).

[47b] [2016] EWHC 2584 (Pat).

Lack of "technical contribution"/"AgrEvo obviousness"/"Plausibility"

Add new paragraph:

12-43a   In *Merck Sharpe Dohme Ltd v Shionogi & Co Ltd*,[53a] Arnold J rejected the submission that where a claim included a functional limitation, no objection of AgrEvo obviousness could arise.

[53a] [2016] EWHC 2989, 185.

Replace paragraph with:

12-46   The test for plausibility is therefore a threshold test, and it would appear that the standard required in the circumstances in *HGS v Lilly* (a product claim) is comparatively low. See also *Idenix Pharmaceuticals v Gilead*.[55a] In *Idenix*, Kitchin LJ reiterated that the test for plausibility was a low threshold test,[55b] stating that when considering whether a technical effect is plausible in the light of the teaching of the specification and the common general knowledge what must be shown is "a real reason for supposing that the claimed invention will indeed have the promised technical effect".

[55a] [2016] EWCA Civ 1089.

[55b] [2016] EWCA Civ 1089, at [113]–[114]. See also *Warner-Lambert Company LLC v Generics (UK) Inc* [2016] EWCA Civ 1006 (cited by Kitchin LJ in *Idenix*).

Add new paragraph:

12-49a *Merck v Ono* and *Actavis v Lilly* were considered and applied by Birss J in *Actavis Group PTC v ICOS Corp*[58a] and by Henry Carr J in *GSK UK Ltd v Wyeth Holdings LLC.*[58b]

[58a] [2016] EWHC 1955 (Pat), [231]–[233].

[58b] [2016] EWHC 1045 (Ch).

3. STRUCTURED APPROACHES TO OBVIOUSNESS

The "problem-solution" approach in the EPO compared with Windsurfing/Pozzoli

Replace paragraph with:

12-90 It may also be noted that the problem/solution approach does not expressly include anything corresponding to *Windsurfing/Pozzoli* step 1, namely identifying the person skilled in the art and the common general knowledge. However this must be implicit: the need to consider inventive step from the viewpoint of the skilled person is expressly required in EPC art.56 in any event. See also *Hospira UK Limited v Genentec Inc.*[105a]

[105a] [2016] EWCA Civ 780, [15].

Add new paragraph:

12-93a In rejecting a mechanistic approach see the two *Hospira UK Limited v Genentec Inc* cases in the Court of Appeal in 2016.[108a]

[108a] [2016] EWCA Civ 780, [15] and [2016] EWCA Civ 1185, [45].

4. EVIDENCE RELATING TO OBVIOUSNESS

Secondary evidence

Replace fn.118 with:

[118] [2010] EWCA Civ 819, [84]–[85] applied by Henry Carr J in *Hospira UK Ltd v Cubist Pharmaceuticals Ltd* [2016] EWHC 1285 (Pat).

Add new paragraph:

12-104a The roll of secondary evidence has been considered in *Hospira UK Ltd v Cubist Pharmaceuticals Ltd,*[119a] and in *Positec Power Tools Europe Ltd v Husqvarna AB*[119b] (in the context of a disclosure application).

[119a] [2016] EWHC 1285 (Pat).

[119b] [2016] EWHC 1061 (Pat).

Disclosure relating to secondary evidence

Replace paragraph with:

12-123 The law and practice of disclosure of inventor's records was reviewed by the Court of Appeal in *Nichia v Argos.*[148] In a dissenting judgment, Jacob LJ reviewed the authorities and noted that cases where such disclosure made any significant difference to the overall outcome were rare. However, the majority considered that it was wrong to impose a blanket rule of no disclosure, but that considerations of proportionality should guide any search. In *Positec Power Tools Europe Ltd v Husqvarna AB* [148a] the position of this kind of disclosure was reconsidered in the light of amendments to the CPR which had been made after *Nichia v Argos* was decided.

[148] [2007] F.S.R. 38.

[148a] [2016] EWHC 1061 (Pat).

Replace paragraph with:

12-125   The current practice relating to disclosure, including the decision in *Positec Power Tools Europe Ltd v Husqvarna AB* [149a] is further considered at para.19-248, et seq. and para.19-292.

[149a] [2016] EWHC 1061 (Pat).

5.   Relevant Considerations in Assessing Obviousness

Obvious to try

The expectation of success

Replace paragraph with:

12-131   This passage was expressly approved by the Court of Appeal in *Palmaz's European Patents.* [154] In *Glaxo Group's Patent* [155] it was held that if it is obvious to try something for other reasons, there need be no superadded requirement that there should also be some expectation of success. See also *Unwired Planet v Huawei*, at [182]. [155a]

[154] [2000] R.P.C. 631, [48].

[155] [2004] R.P.C. 43, [42].

[155a] [2016] EWHC 576 (Pat).

Add new paragraph:

12-137a   In *Hospira UK Limited v Genentec Inc* [162a] the Court of Appeal made it clear that there can be no lex specialis for claims which include as part of their technical subject matter a therapeutic effect of benefit. Floyd LJ went on to state that the test for an expectation of success is "is a flexible one...based on asking whether there is in all the relevant circumstances a fair expectation of success". The Court of Appeal's judgment in *Hospira* thus also reiterates the point that is no single standard for an expectation of success. For further recent applications of "obvious to try" and "expectation of success" see *Novartis AG v TEVA,* [162b] *GSK UK Ltd v Wyeth Holdings LLC,* [162c] *Actavis Group PTC v ICOS Corp,* [162d] and *Hospira UK Limited v Cubist.* [162e]

[162a] [2016] EWCA Civ 1185, [45].

[162b] [2016] EWCA Civ 1295.

[162c] [2016] EWHC 1045 (Ch).

[162d] [2016] EWHC 1955 (Pat).

[162e] [2016] EWHC 1285 (Pat).

The expectation of success and research-based industries

Replace paragraph with:

The *Johns Manville* case itself involved a low-technology process in an industry **12-138**
that would not be characterised as research-based. Lord Walker's speech in
Conor[163] reviewed the "obvious to try" test, and pointed out the difficulties to which
its application may give rise in high-technology industries. In the course of so doing, he cited an extra-judicial article by Sir Hugh Laddie quoted above. See also
Hospira UK Limited v Genentec Inc.[163a]

[163]   [2008] R.P.C. 28, [45]–[51].

[163a]   [2016] EWCA Civ 1185, [45].

"Obvious to try" is only one of many considerations

Replace paragraph with:

Thus expectation of success, and therefore the "obvious to try" question itself, **12-144**
is but one of many factors that the court will have to weigh.[170] See also *Hospira
UK Limited v Genentec Inc.*[170a]

[170]   For an example of such a balancing exercise see, e.g. *Generics v Daiichi* [2009] R.P.C. 23, at [43]–
[44].

[170a]   [2016] EWCA Civ 1185, at [45].

Hindsight and Ex post facto analysis

The "step-by-step" approach

Replace fn.176 with:

[176]   [2014] EWHC 3857 (Pat), [240]–[241]. The result of this case was upheld on appeal [2016] **12-149**
EWCA 780 (Civ). For another case relating to the step by step approach see *American Science &
Engineering Inc v Rapiscan Limited* [2016] EWHC 756 (Pat).

Unforeseeable advantages: bonus effects

Add new paragraph:

In *Actavis Group PTC v ICOS Corp*[219a] the relationship between the correct **12-183a**
formulation of the legal question to be decided and an alleged bonus effect was
considered.

[219a]   [2016] EWHC 1955 (Pat), [272]–[273].

CHAPTER 13

INVALIDITY DUE TO INSUFFICIENCY

CONTENTS

2. CLASSICAL INSUFFICIENCY

Quality of the product or process enabled

Add new paragraph:

In *Idenix Pharmaceuticals v Gilead Sciences* [40a] Kitchin LJ considered the use of **13-44a** a functional limitation to avoid an insufficiency objection. He repeated at [139] his guidance in both *Regeneron* (at [102]) and *Novartis v Johnson & Johnson* (at [244]) that where there is a claim limited by function, that such a claim is permissible if that is the only way of defining the monopoly. However, one must consider whether the claims embrace products other than those specifically described for achieving the claimed purpose.

[40a] [2016] EWCA Civ 1089.

4. LACK OF CLARITY/AMBIGUITY

Add new paragraph:

In *Unwired Planet v Huawei* [46a] (at [148]–[163]) Birss J reviewed the law on **13-53a** ambiguity as a ground of invalidity including the legislative background, the cases cited above, and the more recent judgments of the Patents Court (Arnold J) in *Sandvik v Kennametal* [46b] and *Generics v Yeda*. [46c] The judgment followed the recent decisions, noting that it can be difficult to construe claims because trying fairly to describe an invention in words is not always an easy task, whereas a patentee should get no sympathy for avoidable obscurity. The task is to distinguish between cases of a fuzzy boundary and a claim which is truly ambiguous. The judgment continues (at [163]):

"The factual circumstances in which such a truly ambiguous claim has been identified so far in the modern law (Kirin-Amgen and Sandvik) are ones which depend on carrying out a technical test to find out if a product or process is within the claim or not. If the skilled person cannot know whether they are carrying out the right test, then the claim is truly ambiguous and therefore insufficient. That makes sense. However, while the principle cannot be limited just to technical tests, after all SmithKline Beecham was not that sort of case, nevertheless it does not apply simply because one can imagine difficult cases to judge at the edge of a claim. When a defendant has been found to infringe, demonstrating that the claim's scope is at least clear enough to work that out, an argument that the claim should be regarded as truly ambiguous is likely to be met with scepticism."

[46a] [2016] EWHC 576 (Pat).

[46b] [2011] EWHC 3311 (Pat).

[46c] [2012] EWHC 1848 (Pat).

5.   PLAUSIBILITY

Add new paragraph:

13-64a   In *Warner-Lambert v Generics (UK) Limited*[53a] the Court of Appeal reviewed the origin of the requirement that a specification should make the invention plausible or credible and at [39]–[46], Floyd LJ drew together the principles to be adopted when assessing plausibility. Importantly, at [47], he rejected any need to align the test for plausibility with that of obviousness. Therefore, in that case claims were invalid for lack of plausibility since the patent did not make it plausible that the drug would be effective for all subtypes of the disease falling within the claims.

[53a] [2016] EWCA Civ 1006.

Add new paragraph:

13-64b   In *Idenix Pharmaceuticals v Gilead Sciences*[53b] Kitchin LJ addressed insufficiency by lack of plausibility. He found at [114] that the same approach should be adopted in considering obviousness and whether a technical effect is plausible. The test was stated as that "there must be a real reason for supposing that the claimed invention will indeed have the promised technical effect."

[53b] [2016] EWCA Civ 1089.

CHAPTER 14

PATENT INFRINGEMENT

2.   GENERAL PRINCIPLES APPLYING TO INFRINGEMENT

Defendant's intention to infringe

Intention in the case of the infringement of "purpose-limited" claims

Add new paragraph:

14-24a   The law on the scope of Swiss-style claims was considered by the Court of Appeal in *Warner-Lambert Company v Actavis* [33a] and is considered at para.9-283. Floyd LJ addressed the application of that law to infringement in this passage:

> "212.In *Warner-Lambert CoA* [neutral citation [2015] EWCA Civ 556] I said that a manufacturer who knew or could reasonably foresee that some of his drug would intentionally be used for treating pain would be making use of the patentee's inventive contribution in the same way as a manufacturer who actively desired that result. At paragraph 127 I said that the skilled person would understand that the patentee was using the word 'for' in the claim to require that the manufacturer knows (and for this purpose constructive knowledge is enough) or can reasonably foresee the ultimate intentional use for pain.
> 213. The judge's analysis of the factual scenario surrounding Actavis' marketing of Leceant is undoubtedly comprehensive, but I think Mr Miller is correct in saying that in deciding whether there was intentional use for pain the judge considered the state of mind of the three participants in the process, namely the prescribing doctor, the pharmacist, and the patient.
> 214. So far as the doctor was concerned, the judge concluded that the necessary intention was not present. It has to be remembered that the necessary intention was that Actavis' product Lecaent should intentionally be used for pain. There was no doubt that doctors intended the drug pregabalin to be used for pain. However doctors would either prescribe Lyrica, Warner-Lambert's branded product, which could not give rise to infringement, or prescribe generically, in which case the doctor would not know whether the pharmacist would dispense Lyrica or Lecaent.
> 215. Turning to the pharmacist the judge held that he would not normally have the necessary intention either. He will simply intend to dispense the drug which is on the prescription. The pharmacist will have the information which the doctor lacks in the case of a generic prescription, namely the brand of drug (Lyrica/Lecaent)

which is to be dispensed, but will lack information which the doctor has, namely the indication for which the drug was prescribed. Turning to the patient, the judge held that the patient's intention was not relevant. The patient intended to take whatever drug the doctor had prescribed for whatever condition the doctor had prescribed it for.

216. I think the judge fell into error in seeking to dissect the requirement for intentional treatment of pain in this way. Because claims in this form rely for their novelty on the purpose of the use of the drug, it is only essential that the manufacturer is able to foresee that there will be intentional use for the new medical indication. Intentional use is to be distinguished from use where the drug is prescribed for a different indication and, without it in any sense being the intention of the treatment, a pain condition is in fact treated.

217. The issue which the judge was called upon to decide was whether Actavis knew or could foresee that at least some of the prescriptions written generically for pregabalin to treat pain would in fact be fulfilled with Lecaent. Had Warner-Lambert succeeded in upholding valid claims on which they relied for infringement, it would then have been necessary to decide whether, at any of the various dates analysed by the judge, that test of knowledge or foresight was satisfied. If so the judge should have gone on to consider whether Actavis had taken all reasonable steps in their power to prevent Lecaent from being used to treat pain."

[33a] [2016] EWCA Civ 1006.

Onus of proof

Infringement de minimis

Add new paragraph:

14-39a In *NAPP Pharmaceutical Holdings Ltd v Dr Reddy's Laboratories (UK) Ltd*[55a] Arnold J reviewed the law on the application of the de minimis principle to patent infringement. He summarised the general principles as follows (at [136]–[137]):

"136. The *de minimis* principle. There is a general principle of English law (and indeed of most developed legal systems) which is encapsulated in the Latin maxim de minimis non curat lex (the law does not concern itself with trifling matters). More specifically, there is a well-established principle of statutory construction which is expressed in Halsbury's Laws of England (5th ed), vol. 96 at §1143 as follows (footnotes omitted): 'Unless the contrary intention appears, an enactment by implication imports the principle of legal policy expressed in the maxim de minimis non curat ...; so if an enactment is expressed to apply to matters of a certain description it will not apply where the description is satisfied only to a very small extent.'

137. As Lord Dyson remarked in *R (Alvi) v Secretary of State for the Home Department* [2012] UKSC 33, [2012] 1 WLR 2208, an immigration case, at [88], '[i]t goes without saying that the principle de minimis non curat lex (the law is not concerned with very small things) applies in the present context as in most others.' As Lord Phillips of Matravers stated in *Sienkiewicz v Greif (UK) Ltd* [2011] UKSC 10, [2011] 2 AC 229 at [108]: 'I doubt whether it is ever possible to define, in quantitative terms, what for the purposes of the application of any principle of law is de minimis. This must be a question for the judge on the facts of the particular case.'"

[55a] [2016] EWHC 1517 (Pat).

Add new paragraph:

14-39b Arnold J then noted that the application of the de minimis principle to patent law has proved surprisingly controversial (see [138] of *Napp v Dr Reddy's*[55b]) and reviewed the existing authorities as follows:

"139. In *Hoechst Celanese Corp v BP Chemicals Ltd* [1998] FSR 586 the patent in suit was for a process of making acetic acid by carbonylation of methanol. The claim required that 'there are maintained in the reaction medium during the course of the reaction' specified ranges of reactants. Jacob J construed this as follows:

'25. Hoechst say that this means that the process must be operated to produce HOAc for a period of time within the required parameters. Fluctuation from outside into the forbidden area is not excluded. *Maintained* means essentially running a continuous (rather than batch) process. If there is any significant production of HOAc within the specified parameters, there is infringement. So if on one day the parameters are satisfied, there is infringement on that day, even if on other days (even many other days) the parameters are not met. If there were a momentary "spike" that might not fall within the claim but no one is concerned with that. Even a day's production amounts to 800 tonnes.

26. BP say the words mean that the parameters must be kept within the limits of the claim for a significant period of time in the context of the reaction as a whole. A short term fluctuation into the range will not alter the fact that it is being 'maintained' outside the range. ...

27. The patent gives little explicit guidance on the point. ...

28. I think there are several difficulties with the BP approach. First, over what period is one to take an "average"? Suppose the reactor is run for a year with one or two days of excursion. On the BP approach there is no infringement. But suppose those two days are at the beginning of the year. If one looks just at the first two days, all the operation is within the specified parameters so there is infringement. How (and when) can it cease to be an infringement because for a later period there is operation outside the parameters? Second, the approach is close to introducing a subjective element: at what level did the alleged infringer intend to operate? That cannot be a relevant matter. Third I cannot think of any reason why the patentee would want to exclude any significant commercial production within his specified parameters. Doubtless he would not be interested in truly transient "spikes" but anything as much as a day's production he would surely wish to catch.

29. Accordingly I think Hoechst are right on this point. Since the measurements were taken daily, I propose to approach the question of infringement on the basis that, if, on any particular day, BP were within the parameters, they infringed on that day.'

140. The first point to note about this passage is that Jacob J did not, at least explicitly, consider the application of the de minimis principle, presumably because BP did not rely on that principle. The second point is that this is understandable given that the available data consisted of daily measurements, and that a single day's production amounted to 800 tonnes, a substantial quantity on any view. The third point is that Jacob J was concerned with an allegation of historic infringement which Hoechst accepted had come to an end (see [1]), and both sides had adduced extensive evidence about the BP process conditions over the whole period of alleged infringement (see [59]). Thus the claim was the exact opposite of a quia timet case.

141. In *Monsanto Technology LLC v Cargill International SA* [2007] EWHC 2257 (Pat), [2008] FSR 7 the patent in suit was concerned with enzymes called EPSPS enzymes which, if expressed in a plant, conferred resistance to the herbicide round up. Claim 1 was to an isolated DNA sequence encoding an EPSPS enzyme,

claim 4 (using the numbering after amendment) was to a recombinant double-stranded DNA molecule having particular characteristics, claim 5 was a method claim corresponding to claim 4 and claim 6 was to a plant cell comprising a DNA molecule of claim 4. The allegation of infringement concerned 5000 tonnes of soya bean meal shipped on the MV Podhale to the United Kingdom. The meal had been made from soya beans grown from seed carrying the gene for one of the EPSPSs disclosed in the patent. Pumfrey J found as a fact that there was present in the meal some genomic DNA which included the EPSPS gene and that some or all of that DNA was double-stranded. He nevertheless held that the allegations of infringement failed for various reasons. He added at [89]: 'I should also deal with a de minimis point. The DNA present in the meal, such as it is, is entirely irrelevant to the meal as an animal feedstuff, is present in small, variable, quantities and may not be present at all if processing conditions are changed. It is not in any serious sense genetic material. It is just the remains of the material which was in the soybeans from which the meal was extracted. This, it seems to me, is irrelevant. It may raise a question on damages, that there is no causative relationship between acts of infringement, as opposed to acts which are not infringing by English law, and the loss suffered by Monsanto, but this was not argued. There is, generally, no authority in favour of trace quantities of infringing material being held not to infringe, and some authority against it. In any event, I had no proper estimate of the quantity of DNA in the Podhale meal that survived: Professor Lichtenstein put it at 5 per cent of the DNA in cross-examination but the issue was not properly pleaded.'

142. It is not clear what Pumfrey J had in mind when he said there was 'some authority against' 'trace quantities of infringing material being held not to infringe', although it may have been *Hoechst v BP*. Be that as it may, if the 5% estimate was accurate, that would have meant that 250 tonnes of meal contained potentially infringing DNA.

143. In *Napp Pharmaceutical Holdings Ltd v Ratiopharm GmbH* [2009] EWCA Civ 252, [2009] RPC 18 one of the patents in suit was to 'a controlled release oxycodone dosage form... wherein said dosage form has an in vitro dissolution rate, when measured by the USP Paddle method' of specified amounts. The USP method was described in the US Pharmacopeia. This described acceptance tests which involved testing at least 6 tablets and possibly up to 24 tablets. There was an issue of construction as to whether the claim called for the whole procedure described in the USP to be carried out, including the acceptance test, so that the claim only covered what passed the acceptance test, or whether it was sufficient that an individual dosage form passed the test. As Jacob LJ explained at [53], the point mattered because 'only a modest (7%, nevertheless significant) proportion' of the defendants' tablets had dissolution rates within the claim. The Court of Appeal agreed with the judge that the claim on its true construction only required an individual tablet to have the specified rates of dissolution. Jacob LJ addressed one of the contrary arguments at [56] as follows: 'Mr. Silverleaf sought to avoid that construction because, necessarily, a single dosage form would be destroyed in testing it for infringement. He suggested it would be more rational to conclude that the skilled reader would be concerned with a batch, which is what the USP acceptance criteria are aimed at. We do not agree. If a single tablet is tested and is shown to be within the claim, it follows that the defendant has infringed. If some of his tablets are outside the claim, experiments can clearly be run to estimate the scale of infringement. Moreover, Mr. Silverleaf's construction also involves destruction of tablets—and perhaps quite a lot of them. So the destruction point is essentially neutral.'

144. Again Jacob LJ did not consider the application of the *de minimis* principle. Moreover, his comments must be seen against the context that it was not disputed that 7% of the tablets fell within the claim. As Jacob LJ pointed out, that was a

significant proportion. Jacob LJ was not considering what the position would be if, say, a single tablet out of a million fell within the claim. Still less was he considering a claim that, statistically speaking, it could be predicted that one tablet out of a million produced over an extended period would fall within the claim.

145. In *H. Lundbeck A/S v Norpharma Spa* [2011] EWHC 907 (Pat), [2011] RPC 23 the patent in suit claimed a process for preparing a chemical referred to as 5-cbx which involved 'heating the mixture at 120-145°C'. The period of heating was not specified. One of the issues was what happened if the temperature went into and out of the claimed range. Floyd J held that the skilled person would understand that, provided he made some 5-cbx within the specified temperature range, then he would infringe, even if the rest of the 5-cbx was made at a temperature outside the claimed range. He went on at [49]: 'It is arguable that there may come a point where the amount of time that the process is within the range is so small that it can be ignored. Obviously if the time is so short that no 5-cbx is made during that time, then this does not infringe. I did not hear argument on whether there should be a "de minimis" limit and, if so, what it might be. The point is not free of authority: see the observations of Pumfrey J. in *Monsanto Technology LLC v Cargill International SA* [2007] EWHC 2257 (Pat), [2008] F.S.R. 7 in connection with a product claim. As I do not think that infringement by any of the processes with which I am concerned really turn on this point, I say no more about it here.'

146. In *Generics (UK) Ltd v Warner-Lambert LLC* [2015] EWHC 2458 (Pat) I held that Actavis had not infringed the Patent pursuant to section 60(1)(c) of the Patents Act 1977 because it was not foreseeable that the Lecaent would be administered for the treatment of pain 'save in a small number of exceptional cases which I consider that it is proper to regard as de minimis.' I did not consider the application of the de minimis principle in any detail, however, and I did not have the benefit of the citation of authority which I have had in the present case. Furthermore, this decision is presently under appeal."

[55b] [2016] EWHC 1517 (Pat).

Add new paragraph:

Arnold J went on to apply the principle finding on the facts of the case that provided the number of infringing items was less than one in 10,000, then this represented a threshold for the application of the de minimis principle. Accordingly, there was no threat to infringe the patent. His reasoning (at [147]–[149] of *Napp v Dr Reddy's*[55c]) was as follows: **14-39c**

"147. In the present case counsel for Napp accepted that the de minimis principle applied to claims for patent infringement. Moreover, he accepted that, to take an extreme example, if only one patch in a trillion (10^{12}) fell within the claim, then the Defendants would not infringe the claim. He nevertheless submitted that the Defendants would infringe if larger, but still very small, proportions of their patches infringed. By way of illustration, he postulated a scenario in which it could be shown that, out of 2 million patches sold by a defendant between now and the expiry of the Patent, 200 fell within the claim (i.e. 1 in 10,000 or 0.01%). He argued that a defendant who sold just 200 patches which fell within the claim would undoubtedly infringe, and that it made no difference if the 200 patches constituted a single hour's production out of a year's worth of production, nor even if the 200 patches were randomly distributed amongst 1,999,800 non-infringing patches.

148. I can only say that I disagree. It seems to me that most people, and specifically the skilled person, would be very surprised by the proposition that selling products only 0.01% of which fall within the claim constitutes patent infringe-

ment, particularly where the 0.01% are randomly distributed among the remainder. I consider that this is precisely the kind of situation covered by the de minimis principle.

149. Furthermore, while I accept the force of Lord Phillips' warning about the dangers of trying to define a quantitative limit, it seems to me that, for reasons which will become clear, in the present case the court is forced, as a matter of practical reality, to draw a line somewhere. Where that line should be I will consider below. [at paragraphs 211 to 222 of the judgment]"

[55c] [2016] EWHC 1517 (Pat).

3. NATURE OF THE INFRINGING ACT

Indirect infringement under s.60(2)

Knowledge

Add new paragraph:

14-118a   In *Actavis UK Limited v Eli Lilly & Co* [130a] Arnold J had to consider, on remission by the Court of Appeal for trial, the issue as to whether the supply of Actavis' products would constitute indirect infringement of patent if marketed with instructions to reconstitute and/or dilute the products with 5 per cent dextrose solution instead of saline (the so-called "Dextrose Remission Issue"). The Actavis Product was a liquid product which did not require reconstitution, and the Summary of Product Characteristics ("SmPC") specified that it was only to be diluted with dextrose solution. Lilly did not dispute that, if the Court of Appeal's judgment as to the scope of the claims was correct (it is currently under appeal to be heard by the Supreme Court in March 2017) and, if the Actavis Product was diluted with dextrose solution rather than saline, the supply of the Actavis Product did not amount to either direct or indirect infringement of the patent.

[130a] [2016] EWHC 234.

Add new paragraph:

14-118b   Lilly resisted the grant of declarations of non-infringement in respect of the supply of the Actavis Product with instructions for dilution with dextrose solution. Lilly contended that it was foreseeable (and hence obvious) that the Actavis Product would be diluted with saline by some customers (or at least, that Actavis had not proved that it is not foreseeable) even though Lilly did not allege that Actavis were taking any steps to encourage the use of saline. In rejecting Lilly's case and granting Actavis declarations of non-infringement in each of the UK, France, Spain and Italy, Arnold J reviewed the law as follows:

"*Indirect infringement*

27.   It is common ground that, so far as is relevant to the Dextrose Remission Issue, there is no relevant difference between UK law and the laws of France, Italy and Spain with respect to indirect infringement. Accordingly it is only necessary for me to set out the UK law.

28.   Section 60 of the Patents Act 1977 provides, so far as is relevant, as follows:

'(2)   Subject to the following provisions of this section, a person (other than the proprietor of the patent) also infringes a patent for an invention if, while the patent is in force and without the consent of the proprietor, he supplies or offers to supply in the United Kingdom a person other than a licensee or other person entitled to work the invention with any of the means, relating to an essential element of the invention, for putting the invention into effect when he knows, or it is obvious to a reasonable person in the circumstances, that those means are suitable for putting, and are intended to put, the invention into effect in the United Kingdom.

(3) Subsection (2) above shall not apply to the supply or offer of a staple commercial product unless the supply or the offer is made for the purpose of inducing the person supplied or, as the case may be, the person to whom the offer is made to do an act which constitutes an infringement of the patent by virtue of subsection (1) above.'

29. Section 130(7) declares that a number of sections in the 1977 Act, including section 60, 'are so framed as to have, as nearly as practicable, the same effect in the United Kingdom as the corresponding provisions of the European Patent Convention, the Community Patent Convention and the Patent Co-operation Treaty have in the territories to which those Conventions apply.' Section 130(6) provides that references to the Community Patent Convention ('CPC') are to 'that convention as amended or supplemented.

30. Article 26 of the CPC, as revised in 1989, provides as follows:

'Prohibition of indirect use of the invention
1. A Community patent shall also confer on its proprietor the right to prevent all third parties not having his consent from supplying or offering to supply within the territories of the Contracting States a person, other than a party entitled to exploit the patented invention, with means relating to an essential element of that invention, for putting it into effect therein, when the third party knows, or it is obvious in the circumstances, that these means are suitable and intended for putting that invention into effect.
2. Paragraph 1 shall not apply when the means are staple commercial products, except when the third party induces the person supplied to commit acts prohibited by Article 25.
3. Persons performing the acts referred to in Article 27(a) to (c) shall not be considered to be parties entitled to exploit the invention within the meaning of paragraph 1.'

31. The background to Article 26 CPC, and hence section 60(2) of the 1977 Act, was explained by Jacob and Etherton LJJ, with whom Sir David Keene agreed, in *Grimme Landmaschinefabrik GmbH v Scott* [2010] EWCA Civ 1110, [2011] FSR 7 at [82]–[98]. They went on at [105]–[131] to consider the requirements of knowledge and intention in section 60(2). They found helpful guidance in relation to these questions in a number of decisions of the Bundesgerichtshof (Federal Court of Justice) on the corresponding German provision, which also derives from Article 26 CPC. In *KCI Licensing Inc v Smith & Nephew plc* [2010] EWCA Civ 1260, [2011] FSR 8 at [53] Jacob LJ delivering the judgment of the Court of Appeal summarised the key parts of *Grimme* with regard to the requirements of knowledge and intention as follows:

'i) The required intention is to put the invention into effect. The question is what the supplier knows or ought to know about the intention of the person who is in a position to put the invention into effect—the person at the end of the supply chain, [108].
ii) It is enough if the supplier knows (or it is obvious to a reasonable person in the circumstances) that some ultimate users will intend to use or adapt the 'means' so as to infringe, [107(i)] and [114].
iii) There is no requirement that the intention of the individual ultimate user

       must be known to the defendant at the moment of the alleged infringe-
       ment, [124].

iv)   Whilst it is the intention of the ultimate user which matters, a future
      intention of a future ultimate user is enough if that is what one would
      expect in all the circumstances, [125].

v)   The knowledge and intention requirements are satisfied if, at the time of
      supply or offer to supply, the supplier knows, or it obvious to a reason-
      able person in the circumstances, that ultimate users will intend to put the
      invention into effect. This has to be proved on the usual standard of the
      balance of probabilities. It is not enough merely that the means are suit-
      able for putting the invention into effect (for that is a separate require-
      ment), but it is likely to be the case where the supplier proposes or recom-
      mends or even indicates the possibility of such use in his promotional
      material, [131].'

32.   It is clear from these decisions that it is sufficient that a proportion of users will
intend to use the means so as to infringe. Even if the majority of users will not
intend to use the means to infringe, that is only relevant to remedies, and in
particular financial remedies (see *Grimme* at [134]–[137]). On the other hand, one
should disregard 'speculative, maverick or unlikely use' of the means (see
Grimme at [116], [124], [127] and [129]–[130] and *KCI* at [47])."

Section 60(2) and Swiss-type claims

Replace paragraph with:

14-123   In the Court of Appeal in *Warner-Lambert v Generics UK Ltd*, when delivering
the leading judgment, Floyd LJ (with whom Kitchin and Patten LLJ agreed) held:

"Indirect infringement

218.   In *Warner-Lambert CoA* [neutral citation [2015] EWCA Civ 556] I considered
that the case of indirect infringement did not meet the standard for striking out. I
said this at paragraph 138:

'138. ... I consider it is arguable to say that when section 60(2) speaks of "putting the invention into effect", it may be legitimate to look not just at
whether any one person is carrying out the invention in a sense which
would give rise to liability of that person for an act of infringement. It
may be that the invention is put into effect if pregabalin is manufactured
by one person and supplied to another who intentionally uses it for the
treatment of pain. In those circumstances, a person who supplies
pregabalin with the requisite knowledge (i.e. that prescribed in section
60(2) itself) does provide means suitable and intended to put the invention into effect, albeit by the combination of manufacturer and user,
rather than by any one person alone. It may be that this is the reasoning
which underlies the decisions in the Dutch and German cases which I
have referred to.'"

Add new paragraph:

14-123a   At first instance the trial judge held there was no infringement under s.60(2).
Floyd LJ addressed this, starting with a passage from the trial judgment (see [684]):

"684.The fundamental difficulty with Pfizer's claim under section 60(2) remains, as it
has always done, that claims 1 and 3 of the Patent are claims to processes of
manufacture, but there is no act of manufacture by any party downstream from
Actavis, nor even the prospect of such an act. This is so even if manufacturing
(or 'preparation', to use the word in the claims) for this purpose includes packag-

ing with appropriate instructions. In particular, there is no act of manufacture by pharmacists, nor any prospect of such an act. It follows that, although there is no difficulty in concluding that Lecaent's active ingredient is 'means, relating to an essential element of the invention, for putting the invention into effect', Lecaent is not suitable for putting, or intended to put, the invention into effect: either the invention has already been put into effect by the time that Lecaent leaves Actavis' hands or it is not put into effect at all. Accordingly, I conclude that Actavis have not infringed claims 1 and 3 of the Patent pursuant to section 60(2)."

...

"220. Mr Miller advanced two reasons why the claim under section 60(2) could succeed as an alternative claim. The first depended on giving 'invention' a wider meaning in section 60(2), so as to escape the shackles of section 125 which states that the invention is that which is specified in the claim, except where the context otherwise requires. I do not think that argument can prevail in the light of the decision of this court in *Menashe Business Mercantile Ltd v William Hill Organisation Ltd* [2002] EWCA Civ 1702, [2003] 1 WLR 1462 at [24] (Aldous LJ).

221. Mr Miller's second reason built on paragraph 138 of *Warner-Lambert CoA*. He submitted that the process of the invention would be put into effect by the subsequent ascription of purpose by the pharmacist to generic pregabalin supplied by a manufacturer. Although one way in which this might be done was by an express statement on a label applied by a pharmacist, this was not the only way.

222. Mr Speck supported the judge's reasoning. He was prepared to accept, at least for the purposes of argument, that the application by a pharmacist of a label ascribing the patented indication could be an act of manufacture. However, in the absence of any such step, the manufacture was complete at the stage that the product left the manufacturer. Indirect infringement was impossible in these circumstances.

223. On this issue I prefer Mr Miller's submissions. I think there is a danger in translating section 60(2) into a requirement for a 'downstream act of manufacture'. What is required is that means are provided which are for putting the invention into effect.

224. The invention in the present case is the use of pregabalin in the preparation of a pharmaceutical composition for treating pain. As the example of labelling by a pharmacist shows, that process is not completed when the pregabalin has been formulated into a pharmaceutical composition by a manufacturer. The process of preparing the composition can continue through any packaging step performed by the manufacturer and includes the labelling step performed by the pharmacist. I agree with the Danish court's conclusion to that effect in *Warner-Lambert Company LLC and another v Krka d.d. and another*, a case which I do not think was cited to the judge.

225. I have already concluded when considering direct infringement that the significance of a packaging step is only that it demonstrates the necessary intention. I am therefore unable to understand why other acts of the pharmacist in preparing the composition for delivery to the patient cannot also be regarded as relevant acts of preparation, if done with the necessary intention. I cannot agree with the judge that there is no relevant act of preparation by pharmacists, nor any prospect of such an act."

5. STATUTORY EXCEPTIONS TO INFRINGEMENT

Experimental use

Replace paragraph with:

14-179 Similarly, under s.60(5)(b), an act done for experimental purposes relating to the subject-matter of the invention will not be an infringement.

Replace paragraph with:

14-185 Where an infringing product was sold for experimental use by another, the vendor was liable for infringement[227]; it is submitted that the same result would follow under the 1977 Act as it is has been held that seeking to exploit and sell technology cannot be experimental use.[228] To purchase and use infringing articles for the purpose of instructing pupils and to enable them to pull them to pieces and put them together again was not mere experimental use, and amounted to an infringement.[229] In *Meter-Tech LLC v British Gas Trading Ltd*,[229a] Mr Daniel Alexander QC, sitting as a Deputy High Court Judge, construed the subsection as providing for a specific defence, with the consequence that the defendant bears the burden of establishing both that the acts complained of were done for experimental purposes and that those purposes related to the subjection matter of the invention.

[227] *Hoffmann-La Roche & Co A.G. v Harris Pharmaceuticals Ltd* [1977] F.S.R. 200.

[228] *Inhale Therapeutics v Quadrant* [2002] R.P.C. 21, 419.

[229] *United Telephone Co v Sharples* (1885) 2 R.P.C. 28.

[229a] [2016] EWHC 2278 (Pat), [230].

6. OTHER DEFENCES TO INFRINGEMENT

Exhaustion of rights under European Law

Replace quotation with:

14-244 "As a result of the provisions in the Treaty relating to the free movement of goods and in particular of Article 30 [now Article 34 of the TFEU], quantitative restrictions on imports and all measures having equivalent effect are prohibited between Member States.

By Article 36 [ex-art.30] these provisions shall nevertheless not include prohibitions or restrictions on imports justified on grounds of the protection of industrial or commercial property.

Nevertheless, it is clear from this same Article, in particular its second sentence, as well as from the context, that whilst the Treaty does not affect the existence of rights recognized by the legislation of a Member State in matters of industrial and commercial property, yet the exercise of these rights may nevertheless, depending on the circumstances, be affected by the prohibitions in the Treaty.

Inasmuch as it provides an exception to one of the fundamental principles of the Common Market, Article 36 [ex-art.30] in fact only admits of derogations from the free movement of goods where such derogations are justified for the purpose of safeguarding rights which constitute the specific subject matter of this property.

In relation to patents, the specific subject matter of the industrial property is the guarantee that the patentee, to reward the creative effort of the inventor, has the exclusive right to use an invention with a view to manufacturing industrial products and putting them into circulation for the first time, either directly or by the grant of licences to third parties, as well as the right to oppose infringements.

An obstacle to the free movement of goods may arise out of the existence, within a national legislation concerning industrial and commercial property, of provisions laying down that a patentee's right is not exhausted when the product protected by the patent is marketed in another Member State, with the result that the patentee can prevent importation of the product into his own Member State when it has been marketed in another State.

Whereas an obstacle to the free movement of goods of this kind may be justified on the ground of protection of industrial property where such protection is invoked against a product coming from a Member State where it is not patentable and has been manufactured by third parties without the consent of the patentee and in cases where there exist patents, the original proprietors of which are legally and economically independent, a derogation from the principle of the free movement of goods is not, however, justified where the product has been put onto the market in a legal manner, by the patentee himself or with his consent, in the Member State from which it has been imported, in particular in the case of a proprietor of parallel patents.

In fact, if a patentee could prevent the import of protected products marketed by him or with his consent in another Member State, he would be able to partition off national markets and thereby restrict trade between Member States, in a situation where no such restriction was necessary to guarantee the essence of the exclusive rights flowing from the parallel patents."

Delete paras 14-245 to 14-251 inclusive.

CHAPTER 15

AMENDMENT OF SPECIFICATIONS

7.   AMENDMENT AFTER JUDGMENT

Where patent is found partially valid

Directing amendment under s.63(3) and/or limitation under s.63(4)

Add new paragraph:

   In *Idenix Pharmaceuticals v Gilead Sciences*[232a] the Court of Appeal accepted   **15-177a**
without deciding, that the court has a discretion to allow a patentee to retain without
amendment partially valid claims and upheld the refusal to exercise that discretion in the patentee's favour since the case was not one in which the skilled person
would recognise that there was a small subset of compounds which did not have
the required activity. Rather the partially valid claim was systemically deficient and
it would not be in the public interest to allow it to stand unamended.

[232a] [2016] EWCA Civ 1089, [210].

Where patent is found wholly invalid

Add new sentence to end of paragraph:

   This decision to refuse the application as an abuse of process was upheld by the   **15-191**
Court of Appeal.[244a]

[244a] *Generics v Warner Lambert* [2016] EWCA Civ 1006.

CHAPTER 18

FRAND

CONTENTS

5. COMPETITION LAW

Replace paragraph with:

First, it was alleged that there was a failure to ensure a complete and proper ef- **18-42**
fective transfer of an enforceable FRAND obligation. At first instance this allegation, which itself had three aspects, was struck out as being hopeless. [41a] One of the
aspects of this defence was an allegation of breach of art.101 TFEU because the assignment did not transfer the assignor's FRAND obligation to the assignee but
merely required the assignee to commit to FRAND afresh. The basis of this allegation was that the non-discriminatory part of FRAND would now be considered
without reference to the other patents in the transferor's portfolio. The judge held
to have no prospects of success because:

> "It would be unreal and commercially unworkable for competition law to require that the
> transferor's own FRAND obligation should somehow be transferred in the manner al-
> leged by Samsung. That would mean looking back at the position of the transferor in order
> to decide what FRAND terms were today. So many questions arise. Some are the
> following: What happens if the patents are assigned more than once? When considering
> these patents now in the hands of Unwired Planet does one look at Ericsson's portfolio
> today or as it was at the date of transfer? Neither makes much sense when you start think-
> ing about it. How does the transferee or putative licensee get access to information about
> the predecessor's portfolio? What happens when patents are acquired by someone with
> their own existing portfolio?"

[41a] [2015] EWHC 2097 (Pat), [35].

Add new paragraph:

However, the Court of Appeal reinstated this aspect of the defence because it took **18-42a**
the view that in a developing area of law the defendants had a realistic prospect of
persuading a judge at a full trial that in the circumstances of the case, art.101 TFEU
required the effective transfer to the patentee of the assignor's FRAND obligation

so that it could not obtain more favourable terms from its licensees than the assignor could itself have obtained.[41b]

[41b] [2016] EWCA Civ 489; [2016] F.S.R. 35, [47]–[50].

6. CONSEQUENCES OF FRAND ISSUES FOR THE MANAGEMENT OF A TRIAL

Replace fn.45 with:

18-49 [45] This happened in at least *Vringo v ZTE*, *Unwired Planet v Huawei*, *Nokia v IPCom* and *Samsung v Apple*. See also *Seiko Epson v DCI* [2012] EWHC 316 (Pat). In *Illumina v Premaitha* [2016] EWHC 1726 (Pat) the defendant sought to amend its pleadings to raise a number of competition defences. The court adjourned the application to amend until after judgment on infringement and validity.

Add new paragraph:

18-50a The court has the power under the Enterprise Act 2002 s.16(1)(a) to transfer so much of any proceedings that relate to infringement of art.101 and art.102 TFEU to the Competition Appeals Tribunal ("CAT"). In *Unwired Planet v Huawei*,[49a] the court was faced with an application to transfer to the CAT. The court noted that a decision to transfer under s.16 was an exercise of the court's discretion, taking account of all the circumstances, as required by CPR PD 30, and the overriding objective of CPR Pt 1. Saving expense and dealing with a case in a manner proportionate to its value, importance, complexity and the parties' position were all relevant factors. So too was dealing with the case expeditiously and fairly, and allotting an appropriate share of the court's resources to it. A key practical factor was the extent to which a transfer to the CAT would create delay or an increase in costs. The extent to which dividing the issues between the CAT and the High Court might cause difficulties in the proceedings was also important. No transfer should be made without some positive reason for doing so. That requirement did not impose an unfair burden on the party seeking transfer, but reflected that there should be some reason to disturb the "status quo" of the case proceeding where it was. The court refused the request for transfer, primarily because there was no jurisdiction to transfer the contractual FRAND issues to the CAT and therefore transferring the art.101 and art.102 TFEU issues would leave the interrelated contractual claims in the High Court, which would create a division in the handling and decision making process and be a recipe for confusion.

[49a] [2016] EWHC 958 (Pat).

Add new sentence to end of paragraph:

18-52 A further application by the patentee was also refused by the court on the basis that it was not satisfied that benefits of the disclosure requested justified the cost.[50a]

[50a] *Unwired Planet v Huawei* [2016] EWHC 203.

ACTION FOR INFRINGEMENT

CONTENTS

1. THE TRIBUNAL

The Comptroller

Replace fn.12 with:

[12] PA 1977 s.61(5). For the principles applicable see *Luxim v Ceravision* [2007] R.P.C. 33. See also **19-09** *NGPOD Global Ltd v Aspirate N Go Ltd* [2016] EWHC 3124 (Pat).

Stay of court proceedings in favour of EPO opposition proceedings

Replace quoted list with:

"1. The discretion, which is very wide indeed, should be exercised to achieve the bal-   **19-12** ance of justice between the parties having regard to all the relevant circumstances of the particular case.

2. The discretion is of the Patents Court, not of the Court of Appeal. The Court of Appeal would not be justified in interfering with a first instance decision that accords with legal principle and has been reached by taking into account all the relevant, and only the relevant, circumstances.

3. Although neither the EPC nor the 1977 Act contains express provisions relating to automatic or discretionary stay of proceedings in national courts, they provide the context and condition the exercise of the discretion.

4. It should thus be remembered that the possibility of concurrent proceedings contesting the validity of a patent granted by the EPO is inherent in the system established by the EPC. It should also be remembered that national courts exercise exclusive jurisdiction on infringement issues.

5. If there are no other factors, a stay of the national proceedings is the default option. There is no purpose in pursuing two sets of proceedings simply because the Convention allows for it.

6. It is for the party resisting the grant of the stay to show why it should not be granted. Ultimately it is a question of where the balance of justice lies.
7. One important factor affecting the exercise of the discretion is the extent to which refusal of a stay will irrevocably deprive a party of any part of the benefit which the concurrent jurisdiction of the EPO and the national court is intended to confer. Thus, if allowing the national court to proceed might allow the patentee to obtain monetary compensation which is not repayable if the patent is subsequently revoked, this would be a weighty factor in favour of the grant of a stay. It may, however, be possible to mitigate the effect of this factor by the offer of suitable undertakings to repay.
8. The Patents Court judge is entitled to refuse a stay of the national proceedings where the evidence is that some commercial certainty would be achieved at a considerably earlier date in the case of the UK proceedings than in the EPO. It is true that it will not be possible to attain certainty everywhere until the EPO proceedings are finally resolved, but some certainty, sooner rather than later, and somewhere, such as in the UK, rather than nowhere, is, in general, preferable to continuing uncertainty everywhere.
9. It is permissible to take account of the fact that resolution of the national proceedings, whilst not finally resolving everything, may, by deciding some important issues, promote settlement.
10. An important factor affecting the discretion will be the length of time that it will take for the respective proceedings in the national court and in the EPO to reach a conclusion. This is not an independent factor, but needs to be considered in conjunction with the prejudice which any party will suffer from the delay, and lack of certainty, and what the national proceedings can achieve in terms of certainty.
11. The public interest in dispelling the uncertainty surrounding the validity of monopoly rights conferred by the grant of a patent is also a factor to be considered.
12. In weighing the balance it is material to take into account the risk of wasted costs, but this factor will normally be outweighed by commercial factors concerned with early resolution.
13. The hearing of an application for a stay is not to become a mini-trial of the various factors affecting its grant or refusal. The parties' assertions need to be examined critically, but at a relatively high level of generality."

Add new paragraph:

19-15a   However, each case always turns on its own facts and it cannot be assumed that any given set of undertakings will always be adequate to remove the commercial uncertainty caused by a stay. In *Eli Lilly v Janssen Sciences Ireland UC*[26a] the court refused a stay in the light of similar undertakings to those offered and accepted in *Actavis v Pharmacia*. Although the court held that the relative timelines of the UK and EPO proceedings favoured a stay, there were other factors that militated against it. First, there were proceedings for a declaration of non-infringement on foot which neither party wanted split from the issue of validity. The claimant argued that early resolution of the non-infringement issue was important, both so that it could know whether its product infringed, but also so it could know whether the patentee could obtain a SPC based upon a marketing authorisation for the claimant's own product. This latter point would affect the timing of the claimant's application for marketing authorisation. Early resolution of the non-infringement issues would allow the claimant to submit its marketing authorisation dossier confident in the knowledge that even if the marketing authorisation was granted before expiry of the patent, the patentee would not be able to rely on it to apply for a SPC. Secondly, the undertaking offered in relation to damages was only to limit damages to reasonable royalty damages, without specifying a maximum rate for such damages, which was held to increase the uncertainty to the claimant.

26a [2016] EWHC 313 (Pat).

Spin-off value of judgment

Replace fn.27 with:

27 *TNS Group Holdings v Nielsen Media Research* [2009] EWHC 1160 (Pat); [2009] F.S.R 23, see [22]–[26], especially [25]. However, in *Eli Lilly v Janssen Sciences Ireland UC* [2016] EWHC 313 (Pat) the court held at [36] that the "spin-off value" of a decision of the Patents Court was neutral as regards a stay because there might, if the EPO proceedings concluded that neither patent was valid, be a binding ruling which resolved the disputes.

19-16

3.   CLAIM FORM

European cross-border suits

Add new paragraph:

An attempt to avoid the effect of *GAT v LUK* was rejected in *Anan v Molycorp Chemicals & Oxides*. 127a Initially the claimant patentee sought declarations that the UK and German designation of its patent had been infringed by the defendant. When the defendant sought to challenge the validity of the German designation in Germany, the patentee sought to modify its relief so as to seek a declaration that "if the German designation is not invalid (which is to be determined by the German court), it had been infringed by the Defendant". The court rejected this approach for three reasons, each of which came from the decision of the ECJ in *GAT v Luk*. First, the patentee's amendments were a transparent attempt "simply by the way it formulates its claims, to circumvent the mandatory nature of the rule of jurisdiction laid down in that article". Secondly, to allow the patentee's claim to proceed "would have the effect of multiplying the heads of jurisdiction and would be liable to undermine the predictability of the rules of jurisdiction laid down by the Convention". Thirdly, it would "multiply the risk of conflicting decisions which the Convention seeks specifically to avoid."

19-64a

127a [2016] EWHC 1722 (Pat).

Add new paragraph:

A particular type of declaratory relief that has been sought in several cases is a declaration that a party's product was obvious at the priority date of a given patent. Such declaratory relief (often referred to as an "*Arrow* declaration" 127b) is sought when it is desired to clear the way for a product launch but the patent in question has not been granted and the final form of the claims is not settled. *Arrow* declarations are dealt with at para.22-81 of the main work. The UK courts have exclusive jurisdiction over a claim for an *Arrow* declaration as such relief is "concerned with" the validity of a patent because its determination requires the court to determine the single question of whether the party seeking the declaration has infringed a valid claim of such a patent. The fact that it will enable the court to do so pre-emptively before the patent has been granted does not matter. Nor does it matter that the court will not have to decide whether any or all of the claims of the patent will be invalid or whether the product in question will not infringe any or all of the claims of the patent because it will fall outside them. If the court grants the declaration, it will mean that the claims will either be invalid or not infringed, and it does not matter

19-64b

which. Such a claim cannot be characterised as purely concerned with infringement of the patent. [127c]

[127b] *Arrow Generics v Merck & Co Inc* [2009] F.S.R. 39.

[127c] *Fujifilm Kyowa Kirin Biologics Co Ltd v Abbvie Biotechnology Ltd* [2016] EWHC 2204 (Pat) and
upheld in the Court of Appeal at [2017] EWCA Civ 1.

4. INTERIM INJUNCTIONS

Principles governing interim injunctions

Replace fn.164 with:

19-81   [164] *Novartis AG v Hospira UK Ltd* [2013] EWCA Civ 583; [2014] R.P.C. 3. See also *Napp
Pharmaceutical Holdings v Dr Reddy's Laboratories (UK) Ltd* [2016] EWHC 1581 (Pat) where an
interim injunction was granted pending an appeal by the patentee from a decision that the defendants
had not infringed the patent in suit. The court noted at [40] an inconsistency between the indication by
the Court of Appeal in *Novartis v Hospira* that if the Court is satisfied that there is a real prospect of
success on appeal, it will not usually be useful to attempt to form a view as to how much stronger the
prospects of appeal are, and the judgment of the Privy Council in *National Commercial Bank Jamaica
v Olint*, where Lord Hoffmann stated that the relative strengths of the parties' cases was something the
court could take into account.

Types of interim injunction order

Add new paragraph:

19-83a   The court does not have jurisdiction to make an interim order for the provision
of samples for testing for the purposes of obtaining evidence for use in foreign
infringement proceedings. Although art.35 of the Recast Brussels Regulation
permits an application to be made to the courts of one Member State for provisional
measures, even if the courts of another Member State have jurisdiction as to the
substance of the matter, s.25(7) of the Civil Jurisdiction and Judgments Act 1982
excludes from the court's power to grant such interim relief, any interim relief that
relates to the obtaining of evidence. [166a]

[166a] *Anan v Molycorp Chemicals & Oxides* [2016] EWHC 1722 (Pat), [31]–[42].

5. STATEMENTS OF CASE

Defence

(7)   Laches, acquiescence or estoppel

The rule in Henderson v Henderson

Replace paragraph with:

19-179   The parties' desire for a speedy trial on one issue was held to be "special
circumstances" justifying re-opening another issue on an inquiry as to damages on
a cross-undertaking which could have been raised in the main action. [310] However,
a claimant is under no general duty to exercise reasonable diligence to ascertain
whether it has a potential further cause of action against a defendant. [310a] It follows
that a patentee is not required to produce evidence of every type of possible
infringement in a liability hearing, but only sufficient examples so that a case on
infringement could be dealt with in a cost-effective and expeditious way. The
practice of the Patents Court is to allow a patentee who had been successful at trial
to raise further alleged infringements at a damages inquiry or an account of

profits. [310b] Such an approach is also entirely in accordance with the aims of the IPEC, in particular simplifying trials, shortening proceedings and rendering them cost-effective. [310c] If a patentee could have included further infringements in a damages inquiry, it is extremely difficult to see how it could be oppressive for it to include them in a second, subsequent action for infringement instead. [310d]

[310] *Hodgkinson & Corby v Wards Mobility* [1998] F.S.R. 530, CA.

[310a] *AP Racing v Alcon* [2016] EWHC 815 (Pat); [2016] F.S.R. 28, [15]–[21], applying *Aldi Stores Ltd v WSP Group Plc* [2007] EWCA Civ 1260.

[310b] See *Unilin Beheer v Berry Floor NV* [2007] EWCA Civ 364; [2007] F.S.R. 25, [49].

[310c] *AP Racing v Alcon* [2016] EWHC 815 (Pat); [2016] F.S.R. 28, [25]–[28].

[310d] *AP Racing v Alcon* [2016] EWHC 815 (Pat); [2016] F.S.R. 28, [34].

6. CASE MANAGEMENT DIRECTIONS

Handlings cases concerning numerous patents

Add new sentence to end of paragraph:
19-247   The court split a case concerning three patents into two separate trials because of the difference in the priority dates and the subject matter of the patents. [406a]

[406a] *Celltrion Inc v Biogen Idec Inc* [2016] EWHC 188 (Pat).

7. DISCLOSURE

Standard disclosure in patent actions

Product and process descriptions

Add new sentence to end of paragraph:
19-254   Where a party had provided a PPD but was unable to provide information as to a certain claim feature in respect of its product, it was ordered to provide samples so that the product could be tested. [418a]

[418a] *Teva UK Ltd v Icos Corp* [2016] EWHC 1259 (Pat), where the functions of a PPD were reiterated in [22]–[23]. See also *Positec Power Tools (Europe) Ltd v Husqvarna AB* [2016] EWHC 1061 (Pat).

Add new paragraph:
19-254a   A PPD is concerned with is the nature and characteristics of the product or process in issue and the question of whether the product or process falls within the claims, not the factual issue of whether certain acts have or have not been carried out. Therefore, the fact that a PPD has been served in accordance with the rules and practice direction does not alleviate a defendant from the obligation to give disclosure relating to whether it has committed any acts of infringement. [418b]

[418b] See *Varian Medical Systems AG v Elekta Ltd* [2016] EWHC 2679 (Pat), [12]–[16].

Procedure for disclosure

Add new paragraph:
19-259a   Ordinarily a party's obligation is only to give disclosure of documents within its control. However, in *Bristol Myers Squibb v MSD Ltd*, [425a] the court was engaging in an exercise of setting the terms of a license that an infringer could take as a condition for a stay of a final injunction. Because the infringer was seeking a license for the benefit of itself and the other companies in its group, the court held that as a mat-

ter of fairness, disclosure in the license determination proceedings ought to be given on a group-wide basis.

425a [2016] EWHC 2682 (Pat).

Disclosure, requests or questions relating to particular issues

Obviousness

Replace paragraph with:

19-292   The question of discovery in relation to obviousness was reviewed in detail in *Nichia Corp v Argos Ltd*[486] where the Court of Appeal allowed an appeal from a judge's blanket refusal to order disclosure of documents concerning the making of the invention. The judge had held that such disclosure was disproportionate having regard to the secondary nature of such evidence. The Court of Appeal held that such a blanket approach was wrong and a more nuanced approach taking into account the particular facts of the case was appropriate. Notably in that decision Jacob LJ dissented on the basis that in his view the time had now come such the normally such disclosure should not be ordered in a straightforward case. Although this dissent needs to be seen in the subsequent light of the renewed status accorded to so-called secondary evidence in relation to obviousness following the Court of Appeal in *Schlumberger Holdings Limited v Electromagnetic Geoservices AS,*[487] it remains the case that disclosure of documents concerning the making of the invention rarely play any significant role in the outcome of a trial. Disclosure in relation to obviousness was reconsidered in *Positec v Husqvarna*[487a] in light of the changes to CPR Pt 31 arising out of the Jackson reforms. The court noted that standard disclosure was no longer the default option. The court considered in the light of the value of the case, the likely cost of disclosure and the benefits of disclosure of documents recording the making of the invention, both generally and in the specific context of the case. Having done so, no disclosure going to obviousness was ordered. The court justified taking a different approach to the Court of Appeal in *Nichia v Argos* on the basis of the change to CPR Pt 31.5(7). A similar approach was taken in *Illumina v Premaitha.*[487b]

486 [2007] F.S.R. 38. See also *Halcon International Inc v Shell Transport and Trading Co Ltd* [1979] R.P.C. 459; considered in *The Wellcome Foundation v V.R. Laboratories (Australia) Pty. Ltd* [1982] R.P.C. 343; and followed in *SKM S.A. v Wagner Spraytech (UK) Ltd* [1982] R.P.C. 497.

487 [2010] EWCA Civ 819; see para.12-101, et seq.

487a [2016] EWHC 1061 (Pat); [2016] F.S.R. 29.

487b [2016] EWHC 1516 (Pat).

9. EXPERIMENTS

Experiments

Scope of the rule and disclosure of work ups

Replace fn.520 with:

19-320   520 [1999] R.P.C. 154. In *Electromagnetic Geoservices ASA v Petroleum Geo-Services* [2016] EWHC 27 (Pat); [2016] F.S.R. 25, the court emphasised at [10] that the computer modelling and simulations should normally be subject to the experimental notice regime.

Add new heading and paragraph:

The facts to be proved

As noted above, a Notice of Experiments ought (in addition to providing details **19-322a** of the experiment to be performed) to set out the fact(s) sought to be proved by the Notice. The importance of the facts to be proved were explained in *Electromagnetic Geoservices ASA v Petroleum GeoServices*, [526a] where Birss J said this:

> "21. However the order sought by the defendants is not appropriate. Part of the difficulty may have been highlighted by the submission of counsel that the most important fact to be admitted in the Notice was the first one, that when the procedure is followed, the results shown occur. Although Notices of Experiments routinely contain such a fact, to regard it as the most important is to misunderstand the function of that part of a Notice. That fact should normally be the least important fact to be admitted. CPR PD63 7.1 requires that a party seeking to establish any fact by experimental proof conducted for the purpose of litigation must (my emphasis) serve a notice '(1) stating the facts which the party seeks to establish'. This rule is vital for a number of reasons. It requires the party serving the notice to think precisely about what it is that the experiment is supposed to prove and what role it is to play in the case. It gives proper notice to the other party of what facts the experiment is supposed to prove. When the facts are properly set out it should also allow the court to understand what the experiment is for or at least should allow for that understanding to be arrived at fairly readily with further submissions. This in turn allows the court to retain control over the experimental evidence. The permission the court then gives to rely on the experimental evidence is permission to rely on it in order to prove those facts. If the party then changes its case and wishes to rely on the same experiment to prove something different, they may need permission to amend the Notice. That maintains some discipline in the proceedings and mitigates or avoids the problem which arose in *Molnlycke Health Care AB v Brightwake Ltd* [2011] EWHC 140 (Pat); [2011] F.S.R. 26 in which a party wanted to rely at trial on an electron micrograph which had been produced for one purpose for a very different purpose. Taking the approach that the expert's reports explain what facts an experiment is supposed to prove in litigation is not adequate."

[526a] [2016] EWHC 27 (Pat); [2016] F.S.R. 25.

10. MISCELLANEOUS MATTERS

Scientific advisers

Replace fn.548 with:

[548] [2010] EWCA Civ 33. Birss J similarly explained the benefits for the court of a teach-in from a **19-332** scientific advisor in a complex case in *Electromagnetic Geoservices ASA v Petroleum Geo-Services* [2016] EWHC 881 (Pat).

11. THE TRIAL

Expedited trials

Add fn.558a at end of paragraph:

[558a] Considered in *Celltrion Inc v Biogen Idec Inc* [2016] EWHC 188 (Pat). **19-339**

Trial of preliminary issue

Add new paragraph:

19-347a   In *Koninklijke Philips NV v Asustek Computer Inc,* [571a] the question of whether a covenant by the patentee not to sue licensees of a particular manufacturer extended to the defendant's products in issue in the action was tried as a preliminary issue.

[571a] [2016] EWHC 2220 (Pat).

Right to begin

Replace paragraph with:

19-352   The normal rule applies that, unless the court directs to the contrary, the person bearing the onus of proof should begin. Accordingly in patent infringement actions, the patentee will normally begin. Where infringement is admitted and there is a counterclaim for revocation, the applicant for revocation should begin. [576] In *American Science & Engineering Inc v Rapiscan Systems Ltd* [576a] the patentee opened the case. After the fact evidence had been given, the defendant made certain admissions the effect of which was to remove the issue of infringement from the proceedings. The patentee then argued that, as the case was now effectively a revocation action, the defendant should call its expert witness first. The court agreed. It was immaterial that it had previously been anticipated that the patentee's expert would be called first. Further, although the defendant would no longer, if so advised, be able to choose not to call its expert witness, reversing the order of the experts would not deprive the defendant of any legitimate forensic advantage.

[576] As in *Genentech Inc's Patent* [1987] R.P.C. 553, at 558.

[576a] [2016] EWHC 289 (Pat).

Expert evidence

Expert's duty to the court

Add new paragraph:

19-376a   Recently the court has reminded advocates who cross-examine expert witnesses in patent actions to be cautious about criticising an expert witness purely on the basis of omissions from their report unless it is clear that the fault lies with the expert rather than those instructing them. The court also observed that in general too much time is spent by cross-examiners in patent cases on *ad hominem* attacks on expert witnesses that are unfair to the witness, unhelpful to the court and waste expensive time. [614a]

[614a] *Merck Sharp & Dohme Ltd v Shionogi* [2016] EWHC (Pat), [87]–[93].

Duplicative expert evidence

Add to end of paragraph:

19-379   In one case, where each of the two defendants had called their own expert, the court directed that the patentee should put its case in full to the first of the experts to be called. In relation to the second expert, the patentee was permitted to put its case at a higher level, which needed to not be the same level of detail as would have been required if the second expert had been the only witness on a given point. [619a]

[619a] *Unwired Planet v Huawei* [2015] EWHC 3653 (Pat).

Add new heading and paragraph:

Cross examination of the maker of hearsay statements

Where a party serves a hearsay notice under s.2(1) of the Civil Evidence Act 1995 **19-379a** and CPR Pt. 33.2, the other party has the ability to apply under CPR Pt. 33.4(2) for an order permitting it to call the maker of the statement to be cross-examined on the contents of the statement. In *Electromagnetic Geoservices ASA v Petroleum Geo-Services*[619b] the patentee sought to rely on, as hearsay evidence, certain passages from a witness statement of the inventor of the patent that had been served in an earlier action concerning the patent. The defendant sought permission to cross-examine the inventor and wished to cross-examine them on topics that went wider than the evidence the subject of the hearsay notice. The court held that cross-examination permitted by an order under CPR Pt. 33.4 is cross-examination confined to the contents of the statement, although no doubt this could also include cross-examination going to credit. To allow cross-examination wider than the evidence the subject of the hearsay notice was a recipe for confusion. The court observed that there was no doubt that it could, in the exercise of its overall case management powers, permit wider cross-examination in a proper case but to do so would require careful consideration of the consequences.

[619b] [2016] EWHC 27 (Pat); [2016] F.S.R. 25.

Reconsideration of judgment

Add new paragraph:

In *Regeneron Pharmaceuticals Inc v Kymab Ltd*[637a] the court stressed that it was **19-388a** very important that counsel drew the attention of the court to any material omissions in a draft judgment. However, the primary purpose of circulating a draft judgment is to allow typographical or other obvious errors to be corrected, and it is not an opportunity to re-argue the case.

[637a] [2016] EWHC 1177 (Pat), [287]–[288].

12.   APPEALS TO THE COURT OF APPEAL

Permission

Add new paragraph:

In *Teva UK Ltd v Boehringer Ingelheim Pharma GmbH & Co KG*[642a] the Court **19-392a** of Appeal (Floyd LJ giving the judgment, with Kitchin LJ in agreement) considered the extract from the *Pozzoli* case cited above and the observation in this work in the first two sentences of para.19-392. Floyd LJ held at [11]–[13] that:

> "11. Since *Pozzoli*, the rules have moved on. With effect from 3 October 2016 CPR 52.5 provides that the Court of Appeal will determine applications for permission to appeal on paper unless the judge considering the application on paper directs an oral hearing. The judge must so direct where the application 'cannot be fairly determined on paper without an oral hearing'. CPR 52.5(4)(a) provides that the judge directing the oral hearing may identify any issue or issues on which the party seeking permission should specifically focus its submissions in order to assist the court to determine the application. The court may also direct the respondent to serve and file written submissions. Accordingly the court is now placed in a good position to obtain the assistance of the parties. Under these rules,

it would be wrong for a judge to give or refuse permission without being sure that there is, or is not, an arguable point, simply because of the technical or other complexity of the case. It would not be fair to do so. The procedural background is therefore different to that which faced this court in *Pozzoli*.

12. I think the time has come to say that the technical complexity of the background is not a factor which trial judges should take into account in favour of granting permission to appeal. For that reason, there is no justification, in granting or refusing permission to appeal, for treating patent cases any differently to any other cases. In my judgment, the approach in *Pozzoli* should no longer be followed.

13. Nevertheless, Jacob LJ was right that the trial judge, immersed in the technology as he will be, is in a good position to understand whether the case does raise an arguable point for an appeal. This court will always be assisted, therefore, if the judge takes the time to give full reasons for refusing permission, as Morgan J did in this case."

[642a] [2016] EWCA Civ 1296.

Chapter 20

THE INTELLECTUAL PROPERTY ENTERPRISE COURT

Contents

2. Allocation and Transfer Between the Patents Court and IPEC

Replace fn.18:　　　　　　　　　　　　　　　　　　　　　　　　　　　　**20-07**

[18] The relevant transfer provisions have now been considered and applied in a number of cases. Among those not considered separately below are *Caljan Rite-Hite v Solvex* [2011] EWHC 669 (Ch), *Environmental Recycling v Stillwell* [2012] EWHC 2097 (Pat), *Destra v Comada* [2012] EWPCC 39, *Crocuer Enterprises v Giordano Poultry-Plast SPA* [2013] F.S.R. 44, *Canon KK v Badger Office Supplies* [2015] EWHC 259 (Pat), *The Entertainer (Amersham) v Entertainer FZ* [2016] EWHC 344 (Ch), *BG Electrical v ML Accessories* [2016] EWHC 2296 (Pat), and *NVIDIA Corp v Hardware Labs Performance Systems Inc* [2016] EWHC 3135 (Ch).

4. Interim Applications

Case Management Conference

Add new paragraph:

In *AP Racing v Alcon Components* [62a] it was held that the IPEC rules anticipated **20-35a** a split trial between liability and quantum, and that there would be a first case management conference in relation to liability and a second in relation to damages if liability was established. The "exceptional circumstances" rule had to be applied separately in respect of both case management conferences, and the court considering quantum was not excluded from considering further infringements at the second case management conference.

[62a] See [2015] EWHC 1371 (first instance) and [2016] EWHC 815 (Ch) (appeal to Patents Court).

6. Costs

Applicable rules

Add new sentence at end of paragraph:
However, see para.20-42a.　　　　　　　　　　　　　　　　　　　**20-39**

Add new sentence at end of paragraph:

20-41   However, see para.20-42a.

Add new paragraph:

20-42a   In *PPL v Hagan* [75a] the court recognised a tension between the relief under subparas (b) and (d) of r.36.14(3) [75b] and the caps on costs and damages in IPEC. The significance of r.36.14(3) was that where a claimant beats an offer made under CPR Pt 36 it was potentially entitled to costs on the indemnity basis from the date on which the relevant period of the offer expired, and an additional amount not exceeding £75 000. Conversely CPR Pt 45.31 limits costs recovery in IPEC. The court held that the relevant provisions of Pt 36 override the provision of Pt 45, such that the limits on costs in the IPEC (both stage costs and the overall cap) do not apply to an award of costs under r.36.14(3)(b). It follows that a claimant which makes, and beats, its own Pt 36 offer so as to bring what are now subparas (b) and (d) of r.36.17(4) into play can recover more (and perhaps substantially more) than the IPEC caps provide. It should also be noted that old r.36.14(3)(d), and in particular the figure of £75, 000, has now been replaced with a prescribed percentage of 10 per cent of the amount awarded up to £500,000; and (subject to the limit of £75,000), 5 per cent of any amount above that figure. [75c]

[75a] [2016] EWHC 3076 (IPEC). See in particular [28]–[39].

[75b] See now CPR Part 36.17(4)(b) and (d).

[75c] The IPEC can award sums above £500,000 but only where the parties waive the cap by agreement. See para.20-04 of the main work.

Add new section:

8.   THE SHORTER TRIAL SCHEME

20-50   The Chancery Division now offers a Shorter Trial Scheme ("STS"). The scheme is available in the Patents Court. The STS provides many of the advantages of the IPEC procedure but has no limit on the value in dispute. [88] The STS pilot scheme commenced operation on 1 October 2015 and will close to new cases on 30 September 2017. Its procedure has more in common with the IPEC than with the Patents Court, as explained below, hence it is dealt with in this chapter. The STS is not available in the IPEC itself because the similarity in the procedures means there is no need for it. The STS is governed by PD 51N and the following is a summary of its main provisions.

Trials in which the STS is appropriate

20-51   Patent cases may be brought using the STS. That is because the STS scheme is for business disputes and all patent disputes are likely to be business disputes. The STS is not suitable for cases likely to require extensive disclosure and/or reliance upon extensive witness or expert evidence. Lengths of trials in the STS will be no more than four days including reading time. [89] In *BG Electrical v ML Accessories* [90] the court compared this aspect of the STS to the IPEC and concluded that there was little difference between them, as follows:

"The Short Trials Scheme in the Patents Court would limit the hearing to four days, including a time for the judge to read into the case. That would mean probably effectively three and a half days' hearing. In IPEC, although it is usual to have trials heard in two days, it could be three days if I were to think that is appropriate. The difference between three hearing days and three and a half is not, it seems to me, a significant matter. Therefore, so far as complexity is concerned, there is no real difference between the two courts."

All Shorter Trials Scheme claims will be allocated to a designated judge at the time of the first case management conference (CMC) or earlier if necessary.[91] Applications for transfer to and from the scheme should be made promptly and normally not later than the first case management conference.[92] **20-52**

Procedure in the STS prior to trial

The normal rules of pleading under Pt 16.4 are modified as set out in PD 51N para.2.21. There is no requirement to plead arguments, as in IPEC. The particulars of claim, and any defence and counterclaim, should be no longer than 20 pages in length. The court will only exceptionally give permission for longer statements of case, where a party shows good reasons.[93] **20-53**

The case management conference in the STS is in some respects similar to that in the IPEC. For instance the court will review the issues, approve a list of issues, give directions for trial, fix a trial date (or window), and fix a date for a Pre-Trial Review.[94] The STS also has a specific requirement that the trial date or window should not be more than eight months after the case management conference. **20-54**

The normal rules on disclosure under Pts 31.5(2) and 31.7 do not apply but the normal disclosure rules specific to patents, i.e. Product and Process Descriptions, commercial success and validity disclosure, do apply.[95] Any party seeking disclosure must write to the other party not less than 14 days in advance of the case management conference. Any disputes will be resolved at the case management conference. In deciding whether it is necessary to order disclosure the court will have regard to how narrow and specific the request is, whether the requested documents are likely to be of significant probative value and the reasonableness and proportionality of any related search required, having regard to the factors set out in r.31.7(2).[96] Unless otherwise agreed or ordered, if disclosure is to be ordered, the parties will generally be ordered to disclose (i) the documents on which they rely as supporting their case; and (ii) the documents requested by the other party that it agreed to produce or was ordered to produce by the court.[97] **20-55**

At the case management conference the court will consider whether to order that witness evidence and expert evidence should be limited to identified issues or topics. No witness statements should without good reason be more than 25 pages in length.[98] **20-56**

The normal rules for court applications are modified in the STS. For instance, applications (save for the case management conference and pre-trial review) will be dealt with without a hearing unless the court considers it necessary to hold a hearing. Save in exceptional circumstances, the court will not permit a party to submit material at trial in addition to that permitted at the case management conference or by later court order. This is similar to the IPEC's r.62.32(2), save for the addition of the words "or by later court order".[99] **20-57**

At the Pre-Trial Review, the court will review the case and fix the timetable for the trial, including time for speeches and for cross-examination.[100] **20-58**

Trial

20-59 Trials in the STS will be fixed for no more than eight months from the CMC. [101] The rules for the conduct of trials in the STS are similar to IPEC, as follows. The judge hearing the trial will be the designated judge unless it is impractical for that judge to do so. The court will manage the trial to ensure that, save in exceptional circumstances, the trial estimate is adhered to. Cross-examination will be strictly controlled by the court. The trial will be conducted on the basis that it is only necessary for a party to put the principal parts of its case to a witness, unless the court directs otherwise. The court will endeavour to hand down judgment within six weeks of the trial or (if later) final written submissions. [102]

Costs

20-60 There is no costs budgeting in the STS. Instead, the parties each file and simultaneously exchange schedules of their costs incurred in the proceedings within 21 days of the conclusion of the trial (or within such other period as may be ordered by the court). This is to enable the trial judge to make a summary assessment thereof following judgment. [103]

20-61 In the absence of costs management and the summary assessment of all costs the STS resembles the IPEC, but unlike the IPEC, costs in the STS are not capped. Thus costs awarded in the STS may be substantial: for instance, in *Elkamet Kunststofftechnik GmbH v Saint-Gobain Glass France S.A.*, [104] the defendant was ordered to pay the claimant the sum of £458 000 by way of summary assessment.

Appeal

20-62 The Court of Appeal will seek to take into account the fact that a case was in the Shorter Trials Scheme [105] and the desire for expedition in deciding when applications for permission to appeal will be considered and when appeals will be listed.

[88] There is no value limit in the STS. In November 2016 a trial in the STS in the Commercial Court gave judgment for US $ 69M in *National Bank of Abu Dhabi v BP Oil International* [2016] EWHC 2892 (Comm).

[89] See PD 51N paras 2.4, 2.38(e).

[90] [2016] EWHC 2296 (Pat).

[91] See PD 51N para.2.5.

[92] See PD 51N paras 2.10–2.15A regarding transfer generally. Transfer out of the STS was refused in *Elkamet Kunststofftechnik GmbH v Saint-Gobain Glass France S.A.* where the claimant narrowed its case by abandoning reliance on three items of prior art: see [2016] EWHC 3420 (Pat), [7]. Transfer into the STS was refused *NVIDIA Corp v Hardware Labs Performance Systems Inc* [2016] EWHC 3135 (Ch) since the proceedings were too substantial: see *NVIDIA Corp v Hardware Labs Performance Systems Inc*, [47]–[48].

[93] See PD 51N paras 2.22, 2.31.

[94] See PD 51N para.2.38.

[95] PD 51N para.2.39.

[96] See PD 51N para.2.41.

[97] See PD 51N para.2.42.

[98] See PD 51N paras 2.44–2.46.

[99] See PD 51N para.2.47–2.50.

[100] See PD 51N para.2.51.

[101] See PD 51N para.2.38(e).

[102] See PD 51N paras 2.52–2.55.

[103] See PD 51N paras 2.56-2-59.

[104] [2016] EWHC 3421 (Pat).

[105] See PD 51N para.2.60.

CHAPTER 21

REMEDIES FOR INFRINGEMENT

CONTENTS

2. INJUNCTION

Injunction based on threat to infringe

Add new heading and paragraph:

Does clearing the way demonstrate a threat to infringe?

In *Actavis Group PTC EHF v ICOS Corp*[18a] the generic parties submitted that **21-17a** applying to clear the way, with an intention to enter the market if the patent is revoked, is not a threat to infringe the patent. Accordingly, they argued, there was no basis for bringing an infringement counterclaim quia timet. The court held at [346]–[356] that the question was whether there was a sufficiently strong probability that an injunction would be required to prevent infringement. This was first to be examined objectively, and then with regard to the subjective position of the alleged infringer. The court found that there was a sufficiently strong probability that an injunction would be required to prevent the parties from infringing after expiry of the SPC to justify bringing the infringement counterclaim. Birss J held that the inference on which such a quia timet infringement counterclaim is based does not derive solely or even predominantly from the fact they have sought to clear the way by applying to revoke patents. It derives from the marketing authorisation process.

[18a] [2016] EWHC 1955 (Pat).

Add new heading and paragraph:

Napp v Dr Reddy's: no injunction for minimal infringement

In *Napp Pharmaceutical Holdings Ltd v Dr Reddy's Laboratories (UK) Ltd*[21a] **21-19a** Arnold J held that the patent was not infringed but went on to deal with an alternative case lest the matter went further (see [130]–[131]). On the alternative infringement case, he held that injunctive relief would be refused because any infringement was at the de minimis level. However, the judge went on to hold at [168]–[170] that, even if the infringement was not de minimis, an injunction would be disproportionate and a barrier to legitimate trade. It would be disproportionate because the harm to the patentee would be practically indistinguishable from the lawful "harm" arising from non-infringing acts; and it would be a barrier to legitimate trade because the practical effect of injunctive relief would be to require the defendant to operate even further outside the boundaries of the claims of the patent, swelling the patentee's effective monopoly beyond what it claimed, without justification. An appeal on the merits was dismissed by the Court of Appeal at [2016] EWCA Civ 1053 and so these issues did not arise before the Court of Appeal.

[21a] [2016] EWHC 1517 (Pat).

Stay of injunction

Stay of injunction pending appeal

Add new paragraph:

21-36a   In *Fontem Holdings 1BV v Ten Motives Ltd*,[41a] Norris J considered and refused both an application for summary judgment in favour of the alleged infringing parties, and their alternative application to stay infringement proceedings pending the outcome of EPO opposition proceedings. A factor that was relied upon by the applicants for a stay was the "baleful effect of an injunction". The judge held that if infringement were found at trial, then the patentees would only get a financial remedy if a cross-undertaking were offered. However, the judge mooted the possibility that, if an injunction were sought, a further stay could be sought at that stage because of the effect of such an injunction. He cited the "nuanced view" taken in relation to stays of final injunctions pending determination in the EPO by the Court of Appeal in *Smith & Nephew Plc v ConvaTec Technologies Inc.*[41b]

[41a] [2015] EWHC 2752 (Pat): see particularly [34] and [44].

[41b] [2015] EWCA Civ 803.

Add new heading and paragraph:

Seeking injunction on standards-essential patent may be abusive

21-36b   Proceeding for an injunction prohibiting the infringement of a standards-essential patent or seeking the recall of products for the manufacture of which that standards-essential patent has been used may be abusive of the patentee's dominant position if certain conditions are not met: see the judgment of the CJEU in *Huawei Technologies Co Ltd v ZTE Corp.*[41c]

[41c] (C-170/13), Judgment of the Fifth Chamber of the CJEU, 16 July 2015. See particularly [71] and the discussion leading to it.

Add new heading and paragraph:

Injunctive relief following breach of settlement agreement not to infringe

21-39a   Henry Carr J in *Stretchline Intellectual Properties Ltd v H&M Hennes & Mauritz UK Ltd (No.3)*[51a] refused injunctive relief sought by the patentee. The parties had concluded a settlement agreement to compromise an earlier dispute; by that agreement, the defendant had promised not to infringe the claimant's patent. It was later found nonetheless to have done so. The judge held that where a party settled litigation by promising not to infringe an intellectual property right, a claimant should have no more difficulty in obtaining an injunction where that party had broken its word, than where the court had simply found patent infringement in the ordinary way following a trial. The same principles were to be applied to the grant of injunctive relief in the present case as if it been a successful action for patent infringement. Nonetheless, the court refused injunctive relief, since the breaches at issue were historic and unlikely to be repeated. Any further repetition might shift the balance, the court warned, in favour of injunctive relief.

[51a] [2016] EWHC 162 (Pat), [2016] R.P.C. 15.

Add new heading and paragraph: **21-39b**

Non-pursuit of injunction over life-saving products

On occasion, particularly where the alleged infringement is an important or lifesaving medical therapy, a patentee may decide not to pursue an injunction, and merely to seek financial relief instead. In *Merck Sharp & Dohme Ltd v Ono Pharmaceutical Co Ltd* [51b] the claimants were marketing an immunotherapy-based anti-cancer treatment; they sought to clear the way by applying to revoke Ono's patent. Given the life-saving nature of Merck's product, Ono indicated at trial that they would not pursue an injunction, provided that an appropriate royalty was agreed or awarded by the court for future infringements. Similarly in *Glaxosmithkline UK Ltd and Wyeth Holdings LLC* [51c] the patentee did not seek injunctive relief as part of its infringement counterclaim.

[51b] [2015] EWHC 2973 (Pat); [2016] R.P.C. 10: see [2].

[51c] [2016] EWHC 1045 (Ch): see [3].

3. DAMAGES AND PROFITS

Principle on which damages assessed

Extending an inquiry to new causes of action

Add new paragraph:

Mr Justice Henry Carr had to consider an appeal covering a similar issue in the context of a financial relief dispute in the IPEC, in *AP Racing Ltd v Alcon Components Ltd.* [144a] A liability trial and subsequent appeal determined AP Racing's patent to be valid and infringed by certain of Alcon's caliper products. The evidence before Judge Hacon established that there were further Alcon caliper products which at least arguably infringed AP Racing's patent. They were not raised at the CMC, which in an IPEC action is ordinarily the last stage of proceedings at which new points or issues can be raised. On appeal, the Patents Court determined that the practice of allowing claims for relief at the account/inquiry stage for further types of alleged infringements not ruled on by trial court [144b] was entirely in keeping with the practices and aims of the IPEC. The judge found that if it turned out that such an inquiry or account became unduly complicated, it could be the subject of an appropriate order for transfer to the High Court. Accordingly, he allowed consideration of the additional species of infringement. **21-102a**

[144a] [2016] EWHC 815 (Ch), [2016] F.S.R. 28; appeal from judgment of HHJ Hacon [2015] EWHC 1371 (IPEC), [2016] FSR 1.

[144b] Referred to with approval by Jacob LJ in *Unilin Beheer BV v Berry Floor NV* [2007] EWCA Civ 364; [2007] F.S.R. 25, [49].

Principles applicable to an account of profits

Add new paragraph:

21-140a In *OOO Abbott v Design & Display Ltd*,[219a] the Court of Appeal heard an appeal from the taking of an account of profits in the IPEC following a trial for patent infringement. Lord Justice Lewison (with whom Sir Terence Etherton C and Tomlinson LJ agreed) found that the appropriate question of disgorgement was not one with a binary yes/no answer: see [35]. It is open to a judge to find that profits could be recovered in some circumstances but not in others. A key question is whether the infringement "drives" the infringing act. At [36], Lewison LJ said (with emphasis added):

> "Let me revert to the example given by the Full Court in *Dart Industries v Decor Corp* [1994] F.S.R. 567. A manufacturer sells a car which includes a patented brake. If the car did not have brakes, the manufacturer could not have sold it, but it did not have to have that particular brake. In those circumstances the Full Court clearly thought that it would be unjust to charge the manufacturer with the whole profit made on the car; and I agree with them. In my judgment the legal error that the judge made was to ask whether the sale of the panel plus insert would have happened separately rather than to ask himself how much of the profit on the sale was derived from the infringement. In a case in which the infringement does not 'drive' the sale it seems to me that it is wrong in principle to attribute the whole of the profit to the infringement. In particular it does not follow from the fact that the customer wanted a slat wall that incorporated an insert that the customer wanted a slat wall that incorporated the infringing insert. Mr Cuddigan argued that the infringing inserts and the slot were the 'very essence' of the incorporated and unincorporated panels. But the judge made no such finding, and his observations at [32] suggest the contrary. In addition I do not consider that the judge was correct at [31] in saying that 'because the sales went together, the sale of inserts caused ... the sale of the panels...' The mere fact that the two went together is not, in my judgment, sufficient to establish that the whole of the profit earned on the composite item was derived from the invention. One might just as well say that the sale of the panel caused the sale of the insert. As the judge himself recognised the customer specifies panels, and on the hypothesis that he was considering at [31] the customer is indifferent about the inserts (provided that some form of insert is included). On the judge's approach, because the sale of the patented brake went with the sale of the car, the whole of the profit on the car would be included in the account. If the judge had found on the facts that the infringing insert was 'the essential ingredient in the creation of the defendant's whole product' (i.e. the incorporated panel), then he would have been justified, on the facts, in declining to apportion the profit. But I cannot see that he made that finding."

[219a] [2016] EWCA Civ 95; [2016] F.S.R. 27.

Add new heading and paragraph:

Accounts of profits for future infringements? GSK v Wyeth

21-140b At trial in *GSK v Wyeth*,[219b] GSK had been found to infringe Wyeth's valid patent. Wyeth sought financial relief: they sought a damages inquiry or an account, at their election, both over past and future infringements. The court refused[219c] an account of profits for future infringements. An account for future infringements had not been sought in Wyeth's original counterclaim. Additionally, there was no unconscionable element to GSK's future infringements. Indeed, Wyeth had recognised that GSK should be allowed to supply its vaccine, which was in the public interest (this is why it had not sought an injunction: see para.21-39b). In respect of past infringements, though, the judge found Wyeth remained entitled to elect between an inquiry and an account.

[219b] [2016] EWHC 1045 (Ch): see [3].

[219c] *Glaxosmithkline UK Ltd v Wyeth Holdings LLC* (Henry Carr J) Unreported 13 January 2017.

CHAPTER 23

DECLARATIONS

CONTENTS

3. DECLARATIONS UNDER THE COURT'S INHERENT JURISDICTION

A.   Declaration of Non-infringement

Declarations of non-infringement in respect of foreign designations

Add new heading and paragraph:

Rhodia v Molycorp—no contingent declarations of infringement

A related jurisdictional issue arose in *Rhodia v Molycorp*. [84a] Whereas in *Actavis* **23-77a**
v Lilly discussed at para.23-69 et seq., the claimant for the declaration of non-infringement also asked the UK court to consider the corresponding declarations in respect of foreign designations of the patent in suit, in *Rhodia v Molycorp* it was the patentee that was seeking to have both the UK patent and a foreign designation of it (the German) considered together by the Patents Court.

[84a] [2016] EWHC 1722 (Pat).

Add new paragraph:

Rhodia, the patentee, sued Molycorp for infringement of the UK and German **23-77b**
designations of its patent to a ceric oxide product, a method of producing it, and a catalyst for the clarification of exhaust gas. Molycorp acknowledged service without contesting jurisdiction—but as they did so, they also wrote saying they intended to sue in Germany for invalidity of the German designation of the patent. In due course, Molycorp did indeed commence invalidity proceedings in Germany. It was accepted that, as a result of Molycorp's putting its validity in issue elsewhere, the UK no longer had jurisdiction over the German designation in Rhodia's claim as originally pleaded. Rhodia sought to amend its claim so that the infringement issue could still be tried in the UK in relation to both UK and German designations. They sought a declaration that if the patent were not invalidated in Germany, then it was infringed. Rhodia submitted that this avoided the jurisdictional issue, since

[79]

the assessment of that contingent question was not one "concerned with the validity of" that patent.

Add new paragraph:

23-77c   Arnold J did not accept the patentee's position was correct. He held at [24], following *Coin Controls Ltd v Suzo International (UK) Ltd*, [84b] that the material question in issue was in essence a singular one: has the defendant infringed a valid claim of the patent? On that basis, he found that Rhodia's proposed amended declaration still gave rise to an issue "concerned with the validity of [the German designation of the] patent". It therefore engaged art.24(4) of the Brussels Regulation, and therefore the UK court could not entertain jurisdiction.

[84b] [1999] Ch 33; endorsed by the Court of Appeal in both *Fort Dodge Animal Health Ltd v Akzo Nobel NV* [1998] F.S.R. 222, 244–245 and *Prudential Assurance Co Ltd v Prudential Insurance Co of America* [2003] EWCA Civ 327, [2003] 1 W.L.R. 2295, [21] and [23]; and implicitly approved by the CJEU in *Gesellschaft fur Antriebstechnik mbH & Co KG v Lamellen und Kupplungsbau Beteiligungs KG (aka GAT v LuK)* [2006] E.C.R. I-6509 (per Aitkens LJ in *JP Morgan Chase Bank NA v Berliner Verkehrsbetriebe (BVG) Anstalt des Offentlichen Rechts* [2010] EWCA Civ 390, [2012] QB 176).

Add new paragraph:

23-77d   Finally, Rhodia argued that since Molycorp had not contested jurisdiction when it acknowledged service of the claim, it was too late for them to take the position that they had in resisting a trial of the infringement of the German designation before the UK court. The judge dismissed Rhodia's objection, because: (i) the effect of the Brussels Regulation is mandatory on the UK court, and so the Civil Procedure Rules cannot be read to override that mandatory effect; (ii) the jurisdictional issue here did not arise from the particulars of claim whose service Molycorp acknowledged; rather, it came from the nature of the subsequent defence, so the ordinary requirement that jurisdiction be contested before defending the claim could not apply; and (iii) art.27 of the Brussels Regulation would in any event require the court to examine the jurisdictional question of its own motion, even if Molycorp did not take the position it did.

C.   Declaration of Obviousness

Add new heading and paragraphs:

FKB v AbbVie—the Arrow jurisdiction and anti-suit injunctions

23-85a   The existence of the jurisdiction identified in *Arrow Generics v Merck* discussed at para.23-82, et seq., to declare that a given product was obvious at a given date, with the consequence that any subsequent patent to it would be invalid, was confirmed in the Court of Appeal in *FKB v AbbVie*. [89a] The judgment of the Court of Appeal and other judgments in this litigation at first instance all shed light on detailed issues concerning *Arrow*-type declarations and bear detailed consideration below.

23-85b   The patentee's product was a therapeutic antibody called adalimumab. It had been approved for treating adults with rheumatoid arthritis, psoriatic arthritis and psoriasis. The applicant for the declarations intended to market a biosimilar after expiry of the basic patent and SPC covering adalimumab. It sought to clear the way by seeking revocation of two patents to dosage regimens for the use of the antibody in treating a variety of medical indications. The patentee had sought other divisional applications relating to the antibody as well and the applicant in its original claim sought additional *Arrow*-type declarations in the following form: that "products containing a biosimilar monoclonal antibody to the antibody adalimumab for the treatment of rheumatoid arthritis, psoriatic arthritis and/or psoriasis by the administration of 40mg every other week by subcutaneous injection..." would have been obvious at the priority dates of the two granted patents.[89b] The applicant's intention was to forestall any future infringement action by the patentee under any pending divisional applications following their grant. The patentee sought to strike out the applicant's claim for these *Arrow*-type declarations. The strike-out was rejected by the Patents Court (Henry Carr J).[89c]

One of the two patents, "the 656 patent", had been filed in June 2002 and not **23-85c** granted until June 2013. Shortly after responding to fifteen oppositions to the 656 patent, the patentee requested a fourth divisional be granted from the 656 patent ("the Fourth Divisional Application"). Six days after issue of the applicant's claim form, the patentee wrote to the EPO and stated that it no longer approved the text of the granted 656 patent, which was therefore revoked within days. The Fourth Divisional Application was maintained, and was published on the same day that the patentee had written to the EPO disapproving the 656 patent; Henry Carr J held that the two claimed "essentially the same subject matter". The applicant alleged that the patentee acted in this way so as to avoid adjudication of the validity of the 656 patent in opposition proceedings, whilst seeking to prolong commercial uncertainty for potential competitors by maintaining claims to essentially the same subject-matter in the Fourth Divisional Application. The applicant submitted that the patentee was acting so as to frustrate their ability to seek to clear the way for its proposed biosimilar. The applicant relied on this to justify the *Arrow*-type declarations it had sought. The patentee did not accept the applicant's characterisation of its conduct but the patentee's objection to the declarations was based on principle: even if all the asserted facts were true, the court had no jurisdiction to grant such declarations, or alternatively it would be a wrongful exercise of any discretion to do so.

The patentee invited the court to find that *Arrow Generics v Merck* had been **23-85d** wrongly decided, because: (i) such declarations of obviousness are barred by s.74 of the Patents Act 1977; (ii) s.69 of the Patents Act 1977 did not support the contrary position since the declarations were in substance directed prospectively, at the validity of any resulting granted patent from the divisional applications; and (iii) a declaration of obviousness that was framed around the claimant's product, but which was expressed in terms of the features claimed in the applications/patents in suit, amounted in substance to an impermissible request for a declaration (without seeking revocation) that those applications or patents are or would be invalid. Additionally, the patentee argued that there were strong policy reasons for not permitting the UK courts to usurp functions that had been exclusively allocated to the EPO, and that this principle did not depend on the form of the challenge to validity. The patentee submitted that *Arrow* usurped the EPO's exclusive jurisdiction over pre-grant examination of patent validity.

Mr Justice Henry Carr rejected the patentee's arguments, and agreed with the **23-85e** judgment of Kitchin J (as he then was) in *Arrow*. He also rejected the alternative submission that, if the court did have jurisdiction to grant *Arrow*-type declarations, such relief required the presence of exceptional circumstances. The judge considered the ordinary factors relevant to a discretion to grant declaratory relief as being applicable, namely (i) whether the relief sought served a useful purpose; (ii) whether the underlying issue was sufficiently clearly defined; (iii) whether there were special circumstances militating against such relief; and (iv) the balance of justice to the parties. He concluded that the court did have jurisdiction to grant *Arrow*-type relief; that there was a reasonable prospect that the court at trial would exercise its discretion to do so in favour of the applicant, and that therefore the strike-out fell to be dismissed.

23-85f The next step in the litigation was the judgment of Arnold J.[89d] The applicant had started a separate action seeking an *Arrow*-type declaration framed to provide protection against a further application which had not yet proceeded to grant. It concerned the same antibody, but in different dosage regimens and for different indications from those before Henry Carr J. In addition, the applicant sought anti-suit injunctions restraining each of two further companies associated with the patentee from threatening or commencing patent infringement proceedings for acts covered by its *Arrow*-type declaration. The patentee sought to strike-out the action or summary judgment in its favour. Arnold J found that the applicant had a real prospect of success in its claims for *Arrow*-type declarations against the two further companies. He also found that the applicant had a real prospect of succeeding in its claim for an injunction, though he could not see how that would be so if the applicant failed in its claim for a declaration: the claim for an injunction was essentially one to enforce the *Arrow* declaration sought. The judge went on to consider the applicant's application for permission to serve proceedings on the further company based in Bermuda and granted it.

23-85g The Court of Appeal dealt with appeals from both of the first instance decisions referred to above. Both appeals were dismissed; the Court of Appeal unanimously found that *Arrow*-type declarations are available in principle. Lord Justice Floyd summarised the applicable principles (at [98]):

> "i)   A declaration that a product, process or use was old or obvious at a particular date does not necessarily offend against section 74 of the Act.
>
> ii)   Such a declaration may offend against the Act where it is a disguised attack on the validity of a granted patent.
>
> iii) Such declarations do not offend against the scheme of the EPC or the Act simply because the declaration is sought against the background of pending divisional applications by the counter-party.
>
> iv)   On the other hand the existence of pending applications cannot itself be a sufficient justification for granting a declaration.
>
> v)   Whether such a declaration is justified depends on whether a sufficient case can be made for the exercise of the court's discretion in accordance with established principles."

23-85h The power to grant such a declaration is discretionary, and the Court of Appeal held that "it is for the Patents Court to develop the principles for its exercise in more detail" but went on to emphasise its view that "an important factor to be borne in mind in the exercise of the discretion is the existence of the statutory proceedings for revocation, which should be regarded as the normal vehicle for obtaining any desired findings of invalidity."[89e] The Court of Appeal found that Henry Carr J had not erred in his consideration of the exercise of discretion to grant *Arrow*-type relief. As to the appeal from the second action, the Court of Appeal expressed "considerable doubt about whether there will in the end be justification for the grant of an injunction, at least in the wide terms sought,",[89f] but did not consider that at that stage the claim for an injunction should be struck out. The Court of Appeal also upheld Arnold J's refusal to strike out the claim against the patentee UK.

A further judgment in this litigation arose as follows. The patentee informed the **23-85i** applicant that it had de-designated the UK from one patent, that it had informed the EPO that it no longer approved of the text of another patent, and that it was prepared to submit to revocation of the third. The patentee also offered undertakings whose effect, it contended, was that it would obtain no patent protection in the UK that would be infringed by applicant's proposed dealings in biosimilar products. The applicant did not accept the offer and invited the patentee instead to submit to judgment on the declarations, which it declined to do. The patentee applied to strike out the claims as an abuse of process, submitting that in light of the steps it had taken, there was no real prospect that a court could find that the sought-for declarations served any useful purpose, so *Arrow* relief was unnecessary.

In an unreported judgment Henry Carr J held that there was a real prospect that **23-85j** at trial the court would consider that the grant of the declarations sought would serve a useful purpose, namely to frustrate the patentee's ability to create commercial uncertainty for potential competitors considering marketing competing biosimilars. The judge also relied on the potential spin-off value of the declarations, which could influence other European courts and tribunals, particularly in their consideration of preliminary injunctive relief—though the judge doubted that this spin-off value alone would suffice to justify relief. Further relevant factors were (i) protection of the supply chain to the UK and other parts of Europe; (ii) clarity; and (iii) the possibility that such relief would promote settlement.

[89a] [2017] EWCA Civ 1; Longmore, Kitchin and Floyd LJJ (Floyd LJ delivering the Judgment judgment of the Court).

[89b] In fact at the hearing leading to Henry Carr J's judgment [2016] EWHC 425 (Pat) the applicant narrowed the scope of the declaration it sought, but the declaration remained in the same *Arrow*-type form and for the same purpose as the originally-pleaded declaration (see the judgment at [15]).

[89c] [2016] EWHC 425 (Pat).

[89d] At [2016] EWHC 2204 (Pat).

[89e] [2017] EWCA Civ 1, [98].

[89f] [2017] EWCA Civ 1, [107].

ACTION TO RESTRAIN THREATS

CONTENTS

2.   THREATS UNDER THE PATENTS ACT 1977

Nature of threats

Background to be considered

Add new paragraph:
These principles were also applied in *Generics v Warner Lambert.* [49a] Whether a   **24-26a**
communication is a threat depends on how it would be understood by an ordinary
reasonable person in the position of the actual recipient. The ordinary reader will
take into account all of the relevant circumstances known to the parties at the date
of the communication. A communication may amount to a threat even if it is veiled,
covert, conditional or future.

[49a] [2015] EWHC 2548 (Pat) (Arnold J, at [693]).

Add new paragraph:
Some of the communications considered in *Generics v Warner Lambert* [51a] were   **24-27a**
letters to the Department of Health with objectives similar to those in Olin
Mathieson.

[51a] [2015] EWHC 2548 (Pat) (Arnold J).

Factual information, enquiries and mere notification

Add new paragraph:
That a communication did not simply provide factual information about a pat-   **24-34a**
ent was taken into account in deciding that it was an actionable threat in *Generics
v Warner Lambert.* [62a]

[62a] [2015] EWHC 2548 (Pat) (Arnold J, at [710]).

General warnings

Replace paragraph with:
Thus, if, by issuing a general warning, it can be shown that a warning finger was   **24-37**
pointed against the products of some other specific manufacturer, importer or

vendor, the warning becomes an actionable threat. [64] This principle was followed in *Generics v Warner Lambert*. [64a]

[64] See *Weldrics Ltd v Quasi-Arc Co Ltd* (1922) 39 R.P.C. 323; *Cars v Bland Light Syndicate Ltd* (1911) 28 R.P.C. 33; *Boneham and Hart v Hirst Bros Co Ltd* (1917) 34 R.P.C. 209; *Martin v Selsdon Fountain Pen Co Ltd* (1949) 66 R.P.C. 193, 215; *Alpi Pietro E Figlio Co v John Wright Sons (Veneers) Ltd* [1972] R.P.C. 125, 133.

[64a] [2015] EWHC 2548 (Pat) (Arnold J, at [693]).

The claimant

Add new paragraph:

24-43a   In *Generics v Warner Lambert* [77a] a rival generic pharmaceutical supplier was held not to be a person aggrieved by a communication to the Department of Health which itself had been held to be an actionable threat to sue pharmacists, who would have been customers of the rival supplier. That was because the purpose of the communication was to try to put pressure on the Department and the threat was not made with a view to its being disseminated to the persons threatened (pharmacists). It was not capable of doing any real harm to the commercial interests of the rival supplier.

[77a] [2015] EWHC 2548 (Pat) (Arnold J, at [694], [717] and [718]).

3.   JUSTIFICATION

Where an application has been published but no patent has been granted

Replace paragraph with:

24-53   The defence of justification under s.70(2A) is also available, at least in principle, to a person who threatens proceedings for infringement of the rights arising upon publication of an application. [91] In *Global Flood Defence Systems Ltd v Johann Van Den Noort Beheer BV* [91a] Arnold J dealt directly with an argument seeking to distinguish *Brain v Ingledew* and contend that a threat of proceedings for infringement of a granted patent made at a time when the person making the threat only has a pending patent application is incapable of justification under s.70(2A). The judge rejected it, holding that such a threat was capable of justification once the patent was granted. However, in order to sustain the defence it must be shown that the act complained of by the threat would, if the patent had been granted on the date of publication of the application, have infringed the patent as granted. [92] Thus, whether or not the defence can be made out is to be tested as at the date of the trial—not at the date when the threat was made—and if the application does not reach grant by the date of trial then the defence will fail. [93] A stay of the action pending the grant (or final refusal) of the patent is a case management decision and whether such a stay will be granted depends on all the circumstances, particularly the length of time until final resolution in the EPO and the possibility of an interim injunction to protect the claimant in the meantime. In *Brain v Ingledew Brown Bennison & Garrett (No 2)* [94] the court indicated that it would not be appropriate to stay a trial fixed for hearing in a few months' time merely because of the possibility that the patent might be amended in future EPO proceedings since this raised "a whole raft of hypothetical questions". Conversely in *Global Flood Defence Systems Ltd v Johann Van Den Noort Beheer BV* [95] the decision to grant the European Patent had already been taken and it would be granted a week after the second day of the proposed two day trial. In these circumstances the trial was stayed.

[91] *Brain v Ingledew Brown Bennison Garrett* [1996] F.S.R. 341, CA. See Aldous LJ at 348 and Hobhouse LJ at 354–355.

[91a] [2016] EWHC 1851 (Pat).

[92] PA 1977 s.69(1) and (2)(b).

[93] *Brain v Ingledew Brown Bennison Garrett (No.2)* [1997] F.S.R. 271.

[94] [1997] F.S.R. 271.

[95] [2016] EWHC 1851 (Pat).

4. PROCEDURE

Add new heading and paragraph:

Timing of trial of a threats claim

In some cases the presence of alleged threats is a reason for ordering an expedited trial, e.g. *Wirth Research v Fridgeland UK Ltd* [114a] but in others, such as one in which an interim injunction to restrain threats has been granted, the threats action may be adjourned (*Global Flood Defence Systems Ltd v Johann Van Den Noort Beheer BV*). [114b]   **24-64a**

[114a] [2016] EWHC 2857 (Pat).

[114b] [2016] EWHC 99 (IPEC).

5. THE RELIEF

Add new heading and paragraph:

Costs

In *Elkamet Kunststofftechnik GmbH v Saint-Gobain Glass France S.A.* [133] costs were ordered following a consent order dealing with groundless threats. In *Global Flood Defence Systems Ltd v Johann Van Den Noort Beheer BV* [134] all costs were adjourned pending resolution of all issues including a threats claim.   **24-73a**

[133] [2016] EWHC 3420 (Pat).

[134] [2016] EWHC 189 (IPEC).

THE UNIFIED PATENT COURT

CONTENTS

1. INTRODUCTION AND HISTORICAL BACKGROUND

Replace paragraph with:

The Unified Patent Court (UPC) is to be a new court with a more or less pan- **26-01** European jurisdiction in patent matters. The point of the court is to allow European patent disputes to be tried once and for all in one court instead of the current arrangements in which patents are litigated in parallel in many European states at the same time. The instrument creating the court is the UPC Agreement.[1] The court will start to function when the agreement formally comes into force. That occurs when it has been ratified appropriately. Although the UPC Agreement is not yet in force, it is anticipated that the agreement will come into force quite soon. Given the statement by the UK on 28 November 2016 that it will ratify the UPC Agreement, indications are that the UPC may come into full effect at the end of 2017 or early 2018. While many details concerning how the UPC will function are not yet certain, there is sufficient clarity about many aspects to make it possible to address the UPC in this work in outline.

[1] EU Document 16351/12.

2. UPC LEGAL INSTRUMENTS

The instruments setting up the UPC

Replace paragraph with:

The key instruments which set up the UPC system are the UPC Agreement, the **26-25** Protocol on Privileges and Immunities, Regulations 1257/2012 and 1260/2012 and the rules for unitary patents adopted in the EPO.

Add new heading and paragraphs:

Protocol on Privileges and Immunities

The Protocol on Privileges and Immunities[40a] ("PPI") is a protocol which **26-39a** provides for the UPC as an institution to benefit from various privileges and immunities necessary for it to function. For example, art.2 of the PPI provides that the court shall enjoy, in the relevant contracting state, such privileges and immunities as are necessary for the exercise of its official activities. Articles 3 and 4 deal with the inviolability of its premises and records while arts 5, 6, 7 and 8 deal with the court's immunity from legal process, the immunity of state representatives attending meetings, exemption from taxes and freedom for currency restrictions, all subject to various exceptions. Article 9 deals with the privileges and immunities of judges of the court and the registrar, including the internal taxation system, while art.10 deals with the corresponding immunities and privileges of staff. Article 11 is concerned with the court's emblem and flag (who knew the UPC would have a flag) and art.12 provides for co-operation with the authorities of contracting states. Article 13 is concerned with the purpose of the immunities in arts 6, 9 and 10, providing that they are not for the personal benefit of the individuals in whose favour they are granted but are granted in the interest of the court to ensure its freedom of action and independence. Under art.13 the Presidium of the Court shall have a right and duty to waive the immunities of judges and staff if the immunity would hinder the normal course of justice and it is possible to waive the immunity without prejudicing the interests of the UPC. Article 14 provides for rights of entry, residence and departure for judges, the registrar and staff in the relevant contracting state. Article 15 is about notification to states of the names of judges, the registrar and staff to whom the PPI applies whilst art.16 is concerned with dispute resolution. The final arts 17–19 are concerned with entry into force and ratification.

26-39b   The PPI has to be signed by the states with parts of the Central Division (Germany, France and the UK) and the state with the Court of Appeal (Luxembourg) for it to come into force (art.18.1). After the UK referendum on 23 June 2016, Germany, France and Luxembourg signed the PPI on 29 June 2016. Following the statement by the UK on 28 November 2016 that it will ratify the UPC Agreement, the UK announced it had signed the PPI on 14 December 2016.

[40a] European Union Series No.1 (2017) Cmnd. 9405.

EUROPEAN PATENT CONVENTION (EXTRACTS)

Delete heading "Protocol on the Staff Complement of the European Patent Office **AppB-155**
at The Hague (Protocol on Staff Complement) of 29 November 2000".

INDEX

LEGAL TAXONOMY

FROM SWEET & MAXWELL

This index has been prepared using Sweet and Maxwell's Legal Taxonomy. Main index entries conform to keywords provided by the Legal Taxonomy except where references to specific documents or non-standard terms (denoted by quotation marks) have been included. These keywords provide a means of identifying similar concepts in other Sweet & Maxwell publications and online services to which keywords from the Legal Taxonomy have been applied. Readers may find some minor differences between terms used in the text and those which appear in the index. Suggestions to *sweetandmaxwell.taxonomy@tr.com.*

Account of profits
remedies for infringement
principles applicable to, 21-140a—21-140b
Advantages over prior art
unforeseeable advantages, 12-183a
Agreement on a Unified Patent Court
sources of patent law, 1-89
Amendments (specifications)
partial validity
directing amendment, 15-177a
post-judgment
fully invalid, 15-191
Appeals
infringement proceedings
permission to appeal, 19-392a
Applications
supplementary protection certificates
time limits, 6-38, 6-39a
Authorisation
supplementary protection certificates
where authorisation granted, 6-102
Burden of proof
infringement, 14-39a—14-39c
Case management
FRAND undertakings, 18-49, 18-50a, 18-52
Case management conferences
Intellectual Property Enterprise Court, 20-35a
multiple patents, 19-247
Claim forms
cross-border proceedings, 19-64a—19-64b
Claims
Swiss-type claims
indirect infringement, 14-123—14-123a
interpretation, 9-283a—9-283e
Common general knowledge
obviousness
relevant matter, 12-37
Competition law
FRAND undertakings, 18-42—18-42a
Comptroller of Patents Designs and Trade Marks
entitlement proceedings
Comptroller declining to deal with a case, 4-56a
jurisdiction, 19-09
Patent Office opinions
power to revoke, 5-99

Conditions
supplementary protection certificates
authorisation to place product on market granted, 6-102
combinations of active ingredients, 6-150a
medicinal product protection, 6-114a
"product", 6-71a
Costs
Intellectual Property Enterprise Court
rules, 20-39, 20-41, 20-42a
shorter trial scheme, 20-60—20-61
Cross-border disputes
claim forms, 19-64a—19-64b
Damages
infringement
assessment principles, 21-102a
Declarations
declarations of non-infringement (inherent jurisdiction)
foreign designations, 23-77a—23-77d
inherent jurisdiction
declarations of non-infringement, 23-77a—23-77d
obviousness, 23-85a—23-85j
obviousness, 23-85a—23-85j
Declarations of non-infringement
inherent jurisdiction
foreign designations, 23-77a—23-77d
Defences
estoppel, 19-179
exhaustion of rights, 14-244
Disclosure
obviousness, 19-292
procedure for, 19-259a
standard disclosure, 19-254, 19-254a
Duration
paediatric extension of duration of SPCs
application for, 6-182—6-183
Entitlement
jurisdiction
Comptroller declining to deal with a case, 4-56a
"EPC 2000 claims"
indirect infringement, 14-123—14-123a
Estoppel
Henderson v Henderson, 19-179